About the Author

Alasdair Romanes spent 35 years as a French teacher, sports coach, commentator and general factotum in three schools. He now spends his time reading, walking and running slowly. From time to time, he will snap a photograph.

He has written several hundred essays, known as 'Romanes Rants', on a wide range of subjects and one short novel: 'Junk Male'.

For the hundreds of children I have taught and the fun and laughter that they provided. In particular to Joshua who always preferred listening to 'the frog story' rather than studying Latin.

Alasdair Romanes

Frédéric and the Bone Suckers

Austin Macauley Publishers™
London • Cambridge • New York • Sharjah

This is a work of fiction. Names, characters, businesses, places, events, locales, and incidents are either the products of the author's imagination or used in a fictitious manner. Any resemblance to actual persons, living or dead, or actual events is purely coincidental.

A CIP catalogue record for this title is available from the British Library.

ISBN 9781787105690 (Paperback)
ISBN 9781787105706 (Hardback)
ISBN 9781035899883 (ePub e-book)

www.austinmacauley.com

First Published 2023
Austin Macauley Publishers Ltd®
1 Canada Square
Canary Wharf
London
E14 5AA

My heartfelt thanks go to my friend Emma Donald who was so often the guiding and hilarious hand behind my efforts. Grateful thanks go also to another Emma, my niece, who was my first reader – she liked it. To those two excellent Antipodean "Gap Students" Dimity and Lily, thank you for allowing me to borrow your names! Finally to all my pupils who, on rainy days when sport was impossible, listened to me reading this story. My thanks go to the team at Austin Macauley without whose persistence over several years this book would never have moved beyond the files on my computer.

Table of Contents

Prologue

Bone Suckers eat frogs. Fresh. Raw. For years they have met, right in the heart of Paris, underneath the Eiffel Tower. Once the crowds have gone home and the light begins to fade, they furtively edge their way towards a barely visible door in the northeastern corner of the building. In a dark, dingy room, poorly lit by flickering oil lamps, they sit surrounded by upturned crates and discuss new methods for fattening their victims before eating them. Fresh. Raw.

There was, however, nothing furtive about Claude's arrival in their den late one April evening. The short, pale leader of the Bone Suckers burst through the door in a state of absolute fury. Shaking his head angrily so that his filthy, greasy, collar-length hair flew in all directions, he glared around the smelly room before his eyes alighted on his cousin, Clémentine, who was slumped asleep in an armchair, a half-eaten croissant lying on her ample stomach. "Wake up, you fool! Wake up!" He marched over to her and threw an envelope onto her lap. "What do you think about that, eh?"

Clémentine drifted into consciousness. "It's an envelope. More junk mail. Chuck it into the recycling bin; that's what I've done with the rest of them."

"The rest of them? What! You mean you've seen other letters like this?" In his job as a street cleaner, Claude performed his daily tasks wearily but where frog-eating was concerned, he was passionate.

"Yes, Clau, honey," replied his fellow street cleaner and relation, "at least three in the last fortnight. You'd think people had better things to do than clutter up our letterboxes with rubbish, wouldn't you?" Clémentine stuffed the remainder of the croissant greedily into her mouth.

"And you didn't wonder what the logo on the front was about? It didn't strike you as a good idea to examine it before you chucked it away? FFG! It's from the FFG – the Féderation des Fermiers de Grenouilles! The Frog Farmers' Federation!" Claude swiped his cousin crossly on the arm with his black beret.

Clémentine struggled to her feet, one hand sweeping croissant crumbs off her street cleaner's blue overalls whilst the other held the envelope. "Calm down, Clau, it'll just be another circular about frog feed."

"But it's not!" Claude snatched the envelope back and pulled out the letter angrily. "Listen to this, you dimwit!"

"Monsieur and Mademoiselle Malodeur,

It has come to our attention that you have been treating our frogs with outrageous cruelty before eating them. Whilst we are proud of the French tradition of dining on frogs' legs, we cannot condone the methods that you employ any longer and will therefore cease providing you with animals immediately. Enclosed is your final bill of €1,342. Please acknowledge the receipt of this fifth letter and pay what is due before the end of this month.

Yours faithfully
Gérard Maladie."

"So, my little cousin," Claude continued sarcastically, "just how do you propose we get hold of live frogs now? I'm simply not prepared to go to restaurants and eat the things cooked! I have to suck raw frog bone."

A furrow crossed Clémentine's brow. "You're right, Clau. And restaurants serve such ridiculously small portions. No meat on them; no meat at all!" She patted her stomach. "What on earth can we do? It's not as if we can wander around the place looking for wild frogs."

Claude gaped at his cousin. "Clem, you may be a fool most of the time but every now and then you come up with the ideas of a genius! That's precisely what we will do! Blast the FFG! There are wild frogs and we will hunt them. Where do you think those wretched farmers got them from in the first place? And guess what?"

"What? You haven't come up with another of your great plans, have you, Clau?"

Claude grabbed his cousin by the shoulders and gave her a loud kiss on each cheek. "That is exactly what I've done!"

Within days they had adapted their street cleaning trucks and in the early hours of the morning, they jumped aboard them and drove around the roads of France. These machines still swept and sucked up anything that crossed their path – litter, leaves, squirrels and frogs. But now the litter, leaves and squirrels were spat out again; the frogs were not. It worked like a dream. Then in the evenings, purely for entertainment, the cousins, armed with brooms and buckets, wandered around the parks near the Eiffel Tower listening for frogs. Any frog unlucky enough to meet them found itself swept up and a prisoner.

Chapter 1
Pond Life

Not far to the south of Paris was a beautiful pond, which was full of happiness. There, one spring morning a few decades ago, Marie the frog produced a mass of frogspawn. The fish, ducks and insects in the pond were delighted as it provided them with breakfast, lunch and tea day after day. After a couple of weeks, the uneaten spawn began to attach itself to plants and tadpoles began to grow. Before long, thousands of little tadpoles were swimming all over the pond.

Marie was a loving mother and named all of them: Mathieu, Guillaume, Jean and Jeanne, Mathieu, Sophie, Wayne and Christophe, Mathieu and many more. But the fastest and most athletic one she called Frédéric.

Life was not easy for the tadpoles because the fish, ducks and insects loved tadpoles even more than frogspawn. They hunted and preyed on the little creatures remorselessly and soon there were no longer thousands of them. Two hundred and seventeen Mathieus had been eaten and the two hundred and eighteenth had only escaped because, just as he was being swallowed, the fish had let out an enormous burp.

"Crikey, that was a close thing," he shouted to Frédéric. "Hey! Watch out, behind you!"

But Frédéric was never in danger because he was swift and full of tricks. He grasped plants with his tail and changed direction in a flash; he flicked mud into the eyes of his attackers and slapped them on the nose with his rapidly growing front legs; he would even jump clean out of the water, grab hold of a passing dragonfly's tail and hitch a ride, before dropping back into the pond. "You lot are hopeless hunters," he taunted the ducks, "you'll never, ever, catch me!"

He was brilliant and his brothers and sisters were very proud of him. For the first 11 weeks of his life, Frédéric sped unharmed around the pond as more and more of his siblings vanished. But all the time, Frédéric and the other surviving members of his family were changing – first, they had grown those front legs and then back ones and finally, their tails had shrunk until they didn't exist at all – Frédéric and the others were no longer tadpoles, they were frogs. Frédéric gave a celebratory leap and landed on a soft lily pad in the middle of the pond. "Ah, life is good!" he sighed. And, with that, he fell contentedly asleep in the sunshine.

Tadpoles' characters change massively when they become frogs. As Frédéric was lying on that lily pad dreaming of succulent flies and skinny mosquitoes, the electric currents in his brain were busy sparking and flashing so that his mind was altering dramatically and when he woke up Frédéric was different. He saw, surrounding him and the lily pad, a great expanse of murky water. He gave such a shudder of horror that the lily pad wobbled treacherously, threatening to throw him into that water! Just then one of the surviving Mathieus came swimming by. "Hey, Frédéric, cool! We're real frogs! Come and play hide and seek in the reeds!"

In there? thought Frédéric. *In that? No, I can't!*

"I think I'll stay up here, thank you," he replied politely, "I'm enjoying a bit of sun." So Mathieu swam away until he found another Mathieu and together they played hide and seek for hours.

Meanwhile, Frédéric lay trembling on the pad. He was afraid of water! He'd been a tadpole of almost miraculous ability but as a frog, he was a failure. "I can't bear this," he groaned to himself. "What on earth has happened to me?" He was scared and ashamed and began to cry quietly.

Days passed and the other little frogs explored the land around the pond, finding lots of delicious food in the heart of the nearby wood – a few did disappear mysteriously but most returned happily every night. Frédéric, though, was marooned on his small, floating island and didn't know how to reach dry land.

Had he been an ordinary frog, Frédéric would have soon starved but one thing saved him: he was still remarkably athletic. So flies buzzing past, who thought they were well out of range of the sad, strange frog on the lily pad, were whisked out of the air as he leapt high into the sky, sometimes completing a full somersault as he did so!

"Gotcha!" he used to shout, trying to sound carefree. "Gotcha and I'm going to get some more of you." The other frogs began to notice that he never swam and started to tease him.

"Frédéric's scared of the water, Frédéric's scared of the water," sang Mathieu, idly flicking water onto the lily pad.

"You're shivering like a jelly, Frédéric!" jeered Isabelle, "come in for a swim! It's lovely in here!"

"Actually, I'm busy," said Frédéric.

"You're not busy; you're scared and that's why you're shaking. It's pathetic," Isabelle said cruelly.

"If you want to know the truth, I've got a bit of a fever," Frédéric replied.

"Oh really? A fever?" sneered Isabelle. "Come on, Mathieu, let's not hang around here and catch Frédéric's fever. Let's go and find the others and play 'Escape from the Bone Suckers'!"

Frédéric flopped down and began to cry. It seemed that he was trapped forever on his lonely island.

Chapter 2
High and Dry

When Frédéric woke the following morning, the sun was shining and life suddenly didn't seem quite so bleak. *There's no way I'm going to get into the water but I do miss everybody so much,* he thought. *I know, why don't I get them to come and play with me up here instead? Smart thinking, Fred, how clever are you?* He went over to the edge of the pad and peered into the murky depths. "Hey you lot," he called out, jumping up and down excitedly as he spotted some of his brothers and sisters. "Do you want to come and catch some flies up here? It's such fun!" A couple of them glanced up at him briefly and then silently dived deep into the pond leaving nothing but ripples behind them. "Guys," shouted Fred. "Where are you going? Guys?" Frédéric slumped back down unhappily.

For the next few days, he kept inviting other frogs up onto his pad but gradually it dawned on him that nobody wanted anything to do with him; he became more and more depressed.

Marie was worried about her son. "What am I going to do about Frédéric?" she asked her old friend the pike one day.

"What's the matter with him? He seems perfectly alright to me, he's always jumping up and down on that lily pad of his."

"But that's just it! Have you ever seen him anywhere else – like in the water? Actually, do you know what? I'm pretty sure he's frightened of water!"

"What? Don't be absurd," the pike raised an eyebrow quizzically, "he was speeding all over the place not so long ago."

"He's utterly miserable; I swear he hasn't left that wretched lily pad since he became a frog. I haven't seen him in the water once since then. Have you?"

"Well no, not at all, now I think about it. Not even when there's a big game of hide and seek going on. It is a little bit odd; perhaps you're right. So, what are you going to do?"

"Perhaps he's forgotten how to swim? Yes, that could be it; he needs to learn again but it'll be no good trying to teach him in here, it's too deep; he simply wouldn't cope," Marie stared thoughtfully into the distance.

"Isn't there anywhere else you can take him?"

"Hmm, I suppose there is actually. In fact, I know the perfect place; there's a pool in the middle of the wood over there; it's absolutely tiny. If I can just get him there, he'll be able to begin by paddling and in no time at all, he'll be swimming like his father. Have I ever told you that my husband won a gold medal for backstroke at the Olympic games?" Marie still remembered feeling so proud staring up at the medalists on the podium, her husband wearing the gold medal and the handsome Mathieu de Boncorps the silver. "But how am I going to get him to the shore?"

"That's no problem," the pike bared his teeth, "I'll use these. They're not just for show, you know!" The next morning they arrived at Frédéric's pad just after sunrise. The pike gave a quiet cough. "Morning, Frédéric. How are you today?" he enquired politely.

Frédéric ignored him and stared sullenly in the opposite direction. "Frédéric, do you want to come in for a quick dip before the others wake up?" Marie asked. "The water's so calm, there's not a breath of wind. Come on; give it a go!"

"No, leave me alone! I'm quite happy where I am," snapped Frédéric, glaring furiously at his mother. She sighed and then nodded at the pike who dived beneath the surface and used his razor-sharp teeth to bite through the stem of the lily pad. As he did so, the pad wobbled and wavered and Frédéric raised his head in alarm.

"Hey, what are you doing, what's happening? Why's everything moving? Leave my lily pad alone! For goodness sake, you'll have me in the water! Help, Mum, help!"

Marie swam towards him. "It's okay, darling. Don't be worried, we're going to take you to the bank. Everything's going to be alright; I'm going to teach you how to swim again."

"I don't need to learn how to swim; I can do that perfectly well. You don't know what you're talking about!"

"So what is the problem, then?" Marie asked.

Frédéric had stopped listening; he was far too frightened by the water, which was now splashing all over his toes. Whimpering, he curled into a tiny ball in the middle of the lily pad as the pike towed it steadily towards land. Before too long, the pad bumped against the bank.

Frédéric stopped whimpering and slowly opened one eye and peered around. He gave a long sigh of relief and bounded onto dry land with a huge grin on his face.

Marie smiled at the pike. "Thank you. Wish me luck."

"I have a feeling you'll need it," he answered. "He is definitely absolutely terrified of water; I've never seen such a bad case. Let me know how it goes."

Marie went over to where Frédéric was prancing about delightedly. "Well done, Frédéric," she said, "that wasn't so bad was it?"

"No, it was easy! Has that big ugly fish gone now? That fool nearly tipped me into the water. What was up with him? Right! Want a race to that tree, Mum?" he shouted. "On your marks, get set..."

"Just a moment, young fellow! We need to talk because you and I have got some work to do."

"Work? Why work? Work's boring! Come on, just a quick race and then we can find some food. It'll be so much fun, Mum, just you and me having a bit of time together." Frédéric gave a winning smile to his mother.

"We can do all that later but first of all you're going to come with me. We're going to visit a little pool in the wood where we're going to sort out your fear of water once and for all."

Frédéric frowned and then spluttered, "I don't know what you're talking about, Mother; I'm not frightened of water. How can you say I am when I've lived my whole life surrounded by it? Why are you always so mean to me? It's not fair!" With that, he spun around and stalked off.

"Frédéric, come here now!" barked Marie. "Everybody knows you're hydrophobic."

"What are you on about? What's that mean?" Frédéric turned his back towards his mother.

"I've told you. It means you're scared of water!"

"Don't be ridiculous, Mother. Where did you get that idea from? I'm a frog. Frogs love water."

"Oh really! Why don't you ever swim then? If the Bone Suckers come here, you're going to need to swim! Otherwise, they'll catch you in seconds, take you away and eat your legs. Besides, if you're really not scared, why do you always cling on to that blessed lily pad?"

"I don't. I'm always in the water."

"Frédéric!" Marie gave a stern stare. Frédéric was about to protest again but instead, he gave a little sniff, his face crumpled up and he began to cry. "It's alright; we're going to sort everything out. Come with me, I'll look after you." Marie held out her hand gently and, a little reluctantly, Frédéric took it. Together they headed off towards the pool, Marie whispering quiet words of encouragement.

When they arrived, Marie backed into the water, beckoning Frédéric to follow.

"No. I'll drown," he moaned.

"Don't be silly: it's perfectly safe and nobody's watching. Give it a try."

"Must I?"

"I'm afraid you must if you want to be able to escape when the Bone Suckers come and if you want to be a real frog. We'll have you doing backstroke in no time." Frédéric glanced at his mother. He knew she was right. He gritted his teeth and edged towards the water; he really was desperate to succeed. Marie smiled reassuringly. "Well done. Take your time; it'll be fine. You won't be out of your depth at all." Slowly Frédéric placed the tip of a toe into the water. A second toe followed. But then he felt a surge of angry panic and in a flash, he leapt away.

"NO!" he shrieked, white with rage. "I'm not going to do it and you can't make me! You don't get it; I'm not like my father and I never will be. You're always nagging me and telling me I'm not as good as the others. Well, I've had enough. I hate you; I hate this wood and I hate your precious pond."

"Frédéric, behave!"

"Leave me alone! And stop saying Frédéric; my name is Fred!" And with that, he stormed off. Marie followed him for a few paces but then shook her head sadly as he disappeared. He needed some time to calm down.

"I'm not worried by Bone Suckers or even Frog circuses, for that matter. I don't believe they exist anyway," muttered Fred to himself as he stomped through the undergrowth, "there's more to life than water. I'm not going to waste any more of my life hanging around here. I'm going to Paris to seek my fortune. That'll show them!"

Chapter 3
Springtime in Paris

Hours later, Fred was walking dejectedly along a track feeling hungry and alone; perhaps he had made a horrible mistake. He was about to turn back when he heard in the distance the sound of a train. *That's what I'll do,* he thought excitedly, *I'll catch a train!* He hurried on until he reached an embankment next to the railway line. "This is the spot; I'll wait here and jump onto the next one. It's bound to be going to Paris. I'll be there in no time." Ten minutes later a goods train came chugging along. Frédéric steeled himself: it was a long way to jump. He scrambled further up, waited till the train drew level with him and then went for it! For a moment he seemed to hang in the air and then with a jolt he landed on a pile of dusty coal in an open truck. "What a jump! Who needs to swim when you can do that! Paris, here I come!"

It was sheer luck that the train was heading in the right direction. As it trundled through the countryside, Fred practised jumps and tricks; he was feeling happier than he had for ages, *I'm free! No more pond, no more lily pads, no more nagging mother!* he thought with a grin. But as the shadows lengthened he became more apprehensive. "I wonder what Paris is like? Where am I going to live? I'll hop into the first ditch I see and ask the frogs in there where the cool places are." Fred suddenly sat bolt upright. "What if the ditch has got water in it? What do I do then? I wish Mum were here. She'd know what to do. But it's all her fault! She should have left me alone. She made me leave. I'm going to be absolutely fine – after all, I've got this far on my own. Who needs mothers?"

Hours later the goods train drew slowly into a large terminus and ground to a halt. Fred peered nervously over the edge of the truck. It was late evening and the station was almost empty. *Well, I don't see any Bone Suckers,* he thought as he leapt down onto the platform and out into the streets...just as a street sweeper disappeared around a corner. He hopped happily along, searching for a ditch to stay in; occasionally he jumped onto the bumper of a passing car to help speed him on his way through the orange glow of the city. Not long after leaving the station, he found himself on a path flanked by wide lawns. In the distance lay the River Seine but directly in front of him was The Eiffel Tower; he gave a croak of amazement. It was only a little croak - it really was - but it was one croak too many.

Claude and Clémentine had, unfortunately for Fred, just come out of their Headquarters for their evening stroll. The hairs on the back of Claude's ears stood up as he heard the croak: "Over there, by the bin," he hissed to his cousin.

"It's a young one," panted Clémentine who was a little out of shape. "Too small, Clau. Leave it. Not worth the effort."

"Use your head; it's perfect for *The Treatment*," insisted Claude, "I'll get around behind it and drive it towards you."

Slowly he sneaked off, edging along the side of the grass, well away from the central path. Fred meanwhile sat in a trance staring at the Eiffel Tower in front of him. "Sacré bleu! Wow! It's enormous," he marvelled.

Suddenly his sharp hearing picked up the sound of stealthy footsteps behind him. He turned and saw the silhouette of a man looming towards him. Claude lunged. "Caught you!" he cried.

But Fred was too quick and sprang away at lightning pace along the path. Glancing over his shoulder, he saw that the man was now a fair distance away and was falling further behind. "Nobody can catch me! I'm invincible!" Fred laughed, as he gave a giant leap, only to find himself landing not, as he had expected, in the middle of a spacious lawn, but right in the middle of Clémentine's cold, empty, metal bucket. A lid slammed on top.

Fred jumped frantically to try and get out but all to no avail; there was simply no escape.

"Hey, let me out! What do you think you're doing? I'm going to count to five and if you haven't let me go, I'll...I'll...well, you better let me out or you'll be in trouble! One, two..."

"Quiet!" Clémentine shook the bucket. "Or you'll be frog jelly before tea! Tiens! Gosh! – frog jelly – that sounds delicious!"

I feel like jelly already, Fred thought rubbing his head ruefully, "Who are you? I think there's been a mistake. I'm not from these parts; I'm a country frog, not a town frog. You're after somebody else. I'm warning you. Three, four..."

"Enough!" Clémentine swung the bucket against a lamppost; Fred crashed into the side and gave a soft whimper.

"Five..." Fred whispered to himself.

Claude snatched the bucket and marched back towards the Bone Suckers' Headquarters followed by a wheezing Clémentine. Fred was only aware of swinging to and fro, the swaying so severe that it was not long before the little frog was horribly sick.

"Now, where's that key? I'm sure I put it in here somewhere," puffed Clémentine, scrabbling inside her pockets.

"Hurry up, I'm starving; I need to tuck into some food," snapped Claude.

Fred gulped. *This isn't what I came to Paris for,* he thought with a sob, *What if they're Bone Suckers? Oh help, I've got to get out of this mess.*

The dirty oak door creaked open and Clémentine lit a lamp while her cousin put the bucket down in the corner of the dingy room. They sat down to a supper of bread and cheese; quite a lot of bread and masses of cheese in Clémentine's case. Fred gave a sigh of relief and slipped into an exhausted slumber. The meal was washed down with a bottle of cheap red wine followed by coffee so strong that its fumes woke Fred. He had been dreaming that he was back on the green and comfortable lily pad, crunching happily on a water beetle.

"Where am I?" he murmured sleepily. "The bucket!" he shuddered. The two Bone Suckers were deep in conversation, a conversation broken by the occasional loud belch from Clémentine. Fred could only make out one phrase which he heard, uttered with relish, time and time again: '*The Treatment*'. The sound of it filled Fred with terror and he couldn't get back to sleep. Dawn broke: Fred felt the bucket move and then heard the door open.

A minute later he was emptied out of his bucket into a large glass tank. "No! Please, don't drown me!" he screamed in horror as he found himself falling. He landed head first, not in water though, but on a solid floor and he was knocked out completely. The large tank was then loaded into the back of a yellow lorry and the top secured onto it so that escape was impossible.

When Fred regained consciousness, he saw that he was no longer alone. Hundreds of frogs were peering at him. A young frog, hopping eagerly from one foot to the other, fired out questions. "Who are you? When did they capture you? Why do you smell so bad?"

"Ouch!" Fred rubbed his head gingerly. "What did you say?"

"Who are you? When did they capture you? Why do you smell so bad?"

"Do I? Well, you wouldn't smell so good either if you'd been in a filthy bucket for hours! They threw me into it when they finally caught me last night; I was surrounded by thirty of them and I almost got away but they all jumped on me at once."

"Thirty? Are you sure it wasn't a hundred and thirty, Mr Amazing?" came a sarcastic voice from the back of the crowd.

"Well, there were a lot of them anyway and my name isn't Mr Amazing," he blustered, "it's Fred. What do they want with me?"

"It's not you they're interested in; it's your legs, mate," came the same voice, "this lot are the Bone Suckers! We're done for!"

A great wail came from the frightened frogs. "Oh, Hercule, please don't; we don't know that!" whimpered a small frog.

"The Bone Suckers?" Fred repeated. "They really exist?"

"Yes! The greediest, nastiest bunch of frog eaters the world has ever seen. Nobody ever escapes from their clutches. We're all doomed," Hercule gloated. A second wail arose.

"Well, I'm not! I'm getting out of here." Fred began to examine the tank.

"Don't bother, mate! What do you know? You're nothing but a youngster. I told you, we're all doomed."

Fred grew irritated, he hadn't travelled all the way to the capital city to die, "Of course, you're doomed, if you've already given up. Nobody may have got away before but they're going to this time. I don't want to be gobbled up by anyone. I'll find a way. Just you wait!"

"A likely story," sneered Hercule.

Fred turned away and settled down in a corner to think. The small frog crept towards him: "Can I come with you?" she asked.

Chapter 4
Tower of Strength

For three hours, the frogs were driven south. Things would have been worse if there hadn't been lots of food. But the Bone Suckers were already working on fattening up the frogs, so along the sides of the tank were troughs stuffed full of quivering, terrified insects; the frogs tucked in.

The lorry eventually drew to a halt in a lay-by on a long, long, straight road. The back of the lorry opened and Fred saw a man shaking hands with the cousins. Emile's hair and beard were grey and thin, he had a squint and wore unattractive yellow, plastic trousers and jacket which matched the hideous yellow of the lorry. Fred stopped staring at Emile and took in his surroundings. The road was bordered by evenly spaced trees that stretched out into the distance. Next to the lay-by was a tall, white tower reaching, like a lighthouse, high into the blue sky. Beyond it, fields of golden corn spread in all directions with an occasional barn dotted here and there; to both left and right were yet more trees and a line of telegraph poles. On closer inspection, Fred could see that the windows of the tower had been fitted with dull glass and had rusted shut. Fred shivered: there was a trace of evil in the air.

The men unloaded the tank and staggered with it into the tower, followed by Clémentine who was tucking into a chocolate bar. The iron door slammed behind them with a resounding clang. "Still think you'll get out of here, mate?" jeered Hercule.

The lid of the tank was removed and the container was tipped onto its side. Out poured a flood of frogs who were all small; their legs were smaller. Emile smiled at Clémentine and Claude. "I've made a few modifications since you were last here."

"Go on. Let's hear them, then," said Claude doubtfully.

"The frogs still have to climb and jump to the top of the staircase. But I've worked out what to do with the weak ones. Every evening any frogs who haven't made it up to the next step are going to be squashed."

"How?" asked Clémentine, throwing the wrapper onto the floor.

"The front of the step ahead of them slams down," replied Emile, "anyone who hasn't made it to the next step gets squashed under the flap and turns into frog jelly."

"Mmm! Frog jelly! That sounds delicious." Clémentine smacked her lips.

"But what's to stop the frogs who did make it up from jumping all the way back down again?" interrupted Claude.

"Aha! Easy! I've put spikes on the back of each flap. If they try to go back down, they'll be skewered!"

"Mon vieux! Old fellow – it's brilliant!" Claude slapped him on the back.

"Yes and what's more I've built the staircase so that the steps gradually get higher and the muscles in their legs will get bigger because they have to jump further. I've perfected The Treatment!" boasted Emile. "No more measly frogs' legs. Just fat thighs with masses of meat to chew on."

"And all those bones to suck on," drooled Clémentine.

The frogs were aghast except for Fred, who seemed pensive.

"Bravo, Emile! Bravo!" Claude grinned. "By the time they've jumped up all 80 steps, they'll be enormous. And then – chic alors – it's restaurant time!"

The three Bone Suckers spun around and disappeared back through the door, kicking out at the frogs who attempted to follow them. A few of the frogs began to whimper, others broke down into loud tears. Life could not be any worse; death would lurk on every step.

As the door shut behind the three Bone Suckers, Fred sprung up onto the first step and sat down smugly. Ten minutes later a small voice came from below, "Hello up there. We can't get up. How did you manage it?" Fred peered over the edge of the step and saw the small scared frog gazing up at him with big eyes.

"I jumped! It's easy. Have a go."

"We have but the step's too high."

Fred jumped down again. "Okay, I'll help you. What's your name?"

"Dimity," she smiled shyly.

"I'm Fred. Now everybody, bend your knees as much as you can and push off," said Fred who then soared effortlessly back onto the step above. Within moments, Hercule, his friend Gaubert and a handful of other frogs were standing proudly next to Fred but many still remained below.

"Come on, Hercule, let's go on to the next step," said Gaubert, "we'll be at the top in no time."

"Before you do that, have a look up there. Didn't you hear what the Bone Suckers said? We're surrounded by spikes!"

Gaubert leapt upwards to check. "You're right. We don't want to be skewered," he said as he landed back down on the step, "there's nothing more we can do today. I'm going to sleep."

"Good idea," agreed Hercule stretching out on the step next to him and closing his eyes.

"I can't get up!" squeaked a tiny frog.

"Fred," called Dimity, "Cosette and I and lots of others still can't make it up. It's too high."

Down hopped Fred again. "Try a run-up then," he suggested. Soon all the frogs, even little Cosette, had made the leap successfully. Except one. Up sprinted Dimity for the third time and launched herself into space, crashing into the front of the step.

"Ouch, my poor nose!" she yelped, as she slid back down.

Fred thought for a moment. "Wait here! I'll go back up. Try again and, as you jump, stretch out your arms so I can grab you and pull you up." Seconds later Dimity was standing beside Fred and the rest of the frogs; they all danced a little jig of joy.

"Don't forget the steps get higher. It isn't always going to be that easy," Hercule muttered, opening one eye.

"You and I will be okay, mate. Every frog for itself," yawned Gaubert.

"One step at a time, one day at a time. Things can only get better, Hercule." Dimity smiled.

Fred was a superb athlete and, left alone, he would have enjoyed the daily exercise. Others were not such fine physical specimens; they often struggled to come even close to reaching the next level. Fred, however, would seize the edge of the step above and stretch effortlessly down to grab the grasping limbs of those still stuck below. "Going up!" he would say cheerfully. The weaker frogs clung onto him and found themselves flung upwards or given piggybacks to the next step to temporary safety. Fred rallied the fearful, cajoled the timid and even enlisted the help of a few of the more muscular frogs.

The daily slam of the step claimed fewer and fewer victims. The downside to all of this, however, was that the top floor was getting ever nearer and with that came a one-way trip to a restaurant. Death hadn't been outwitted, only delayed.

Chapter 5
The Climb

Day after day the frogs in the tower continued their climb upwards. There were, amongst them, some young orphans whose parents had fallen victim to that curse of all frogs: a kissing prince. A rogue prince was loose in Northern France, planting his lips on frog after frog in the hope that they would turn into a beautiful princess. Turn they did, but none had matched the prince's idea of beauty and each kiss had cost a young frog a parent. These orphans were prone to bursting into tears as they considered how cruelly life had treated them and, terrified though he was of the salty liquid, Fred lifted their mood with stories and jokes. One evening though, when the poor creatures were only halfway up the tower, nothing at all seemed to cheer them up. The prettiest frog walked up to Fred. "I'm fed up with these orphans and their endless crying; they only ever think about themselves. What about a sing-song to cheer me up?"

"A sing-song? Good idea, Lily. That'll do us all some good," said Fred and before long, the two of them had a regular evening show. Lily loved the limelight as she belted out numbers from her favourite musicals. Fred told jokes, some of them not particularly funny but he was French, as were his friends and so all of them found him absolutely hilarious. Except Hercule. He wouldn't even join in when they finished off with a rousing chorus. Whilst Hercule was becoming grumpier, Fred had found a purpose to life and was becoming a kinder and less selfish frog. But even Fred's determination couldn't make the whole climb pass without tragedy. One night an unfortunate sleepwalker wandered off the edge of a step and was skewered down below. Nobody mentioned what had happened but from that day on, Fred and Dimity took it in turns to stay awake at night

Sadly Fred was sometimes so exhausted by the ordeal that there were days when he simply did not have time to save everyone. And so as the height between the steps grew ever greater, the ferocious flap flattened a frog or two or more. Slowly, however, Fred and his friends neared the summit of the tower and finally, on a bright but slightly chilly Thursday, the 80th floor was reached. Lily was first to jump that morning: "That's it, everyone," she whooped, "there aren't any more steps. I've done it, I'm safe!" And she broke into song.

Hercule was the next to jump up and quickly sidled up to her. "Safe, are we? And how do you think we get out of here? How will your hero solve that little problem?"

"Oh no!" she cried. "There's no way out. I'm going to die!" She rushed to the edge of the step. "What have you done to us, Fred? This jumping has been a complete waste of time. We're all going to die!"

"Fred will find a way," came Dimity's voice from below.

"I wasn't talking to you," snapped Lily.

When the last of the frogs had reached the summit, a great cheer rang out and a babble of enthusiastic chatter began. "What happens now then, mate?" challenged Hercule. Each and every frog turned and stared at Fred expectantly, nervous yet excited.

"Well, Fred? I'm waiting," Lily tapped her feet impatiently.

"Give him some time. He'll think of something." Dimity smiled.

Since the frogs had been in the tower Fred had spent a lot of time with Dimity. Whenever things had gone wrong, she would run to him for comfort and seek reassurance. Fred always remained patient and kind when answering her worries and had begun to feel quite fond of this little girl-frog who looked up to him with adoring eyes. But although a solid friendship was forming between Fred and Dimity, it was the beautiful Lily who made Fred's heart beat just that little bit quicker. Fred couldn't wait for the end of each day when he and Lily would sing together. Whilst Dimity was sweet and a great listener, Lily was really stunning with the voice of an angel. Sadly the song that gave her almost the greatest pleasure and which she never dared sing in front of Fred, began: "Alouette, Dimity is so wette." Hercule and Gaubert would always snigger as the tune began and found it hysterical when Lily, behind Fred's back, imitated Dimity hero-worshipping him.

Fred now needed that escape plan and he needed it fast. The frogs didn't know exactly what would happen next but they all knew that it wouldn't be good. As the frogs sat on the 80th floor, he cast his eyes around concentrating hard.

"What's that door over there, do you think?" asked Dimity, pointing at the lift in the centre of the building.

"Shh! Can't you see that he's thinking, Twitty Dimity?" hissed Lily angrily.

"She's so irritating!" whispered Hercule in her ear. "And he's so full of himself. You and I need to ditch those two once we're out of here." Lily stared at him coyly and fluttered her eyelashes.

"Got it," Fred interrupted her train of thought. A broad smile appeared on Fred's face and he nodded to himself confidently as he worked out the exit route in his head. He turned slowly towards them and explained how they were to escape from the room at the top of the tower and shortly afterwards he put his words into action.

"Mind out everyone! Remember, if this is going to work, I need speed," he chirped. He picked up a small pebble and then gathered momentum by performing a series of flick-flacks across the floor. As he reached top speed, he released the pebble which, with a satisfying smash, shattered the window. He sauntered casually to the gaping hole and, as he peered outside, Fred gave a grin of satisfaction. He winked at Lily and seconds later he had leapt out of the window and was flying through the air. "What on earth are you doing, Fred?" Lily squealed.

She need not have worried, for Fred had noticed the wires strung between the telegraph poles outside the tower. He had jumped towards the nearest cable, hooked a rear leg over it and hauled himself onto it. He now carried out a tricky tightrope walk until he found himself within range of a poplar tree. Another huge leap and he was amongst its branches and before too long he was safely on the grass below. He was free.

Chapter 6
Walking the Line

Fred lay down on the grass and stretched out his legs. He looked up at the sky, sighed contentedly in the warmth of the sunshine and breathed in the scent of summer.

"Oi, mate! Enjoying yourself, are you? Don't worry about us, will you?" Hercule's voice wrenched Fred back into the real world: the lovely, gifted Lily, the gentle Dimity and all of his other friends were still stuck in the tower and needed saving. Save them he would. He knew, however, that they were not capable of the huge jumps he had just completed so effortlessly. What they needed was...a bridge. Suddenly, inspiration came to him.

Fred hopped swiftly into the fields, bouncing along with his head popping up at regular intervals above the ripened corn. On the freshening wind, he could hear Hercule's voice, "He's off! Never cared for anyone else! Typical!" Fred smiled to himself.

That's what I need, he thought as he spotted a barn. Inside, in a corner, he discovered a pile of twine, which he picked up in his mouth before racing back to the tree. He scrambled up until he was level with the window. He tied one end of the twine around a sturdy branch and then, holding the other end, flung himself towards the telegraph wire. He tied this end to the wire, creating a narrow walkway, a bit like a tightrope. Fine for Fred to cruise along, but not everyone was quite as agile as he was, so he knew that he had to widen it. Three times he completed the same remarkable trick and then he made his way back to the barn to collect more twine. Eventually, there was a wide bridge of twine from tree to wire and then a second bridge from wire to the window ledge. The time for his frogs to leave their prison had come.

In the hours during which Fred had been building bridges, the Bone Suckers had been pretty active themselves. Back at Headquarters, Claude and Clémentine had been preparing the tank in which the latest group of fattened frogs would be transported from the tower to an exclusive restaurant. In fact, it was Claude who had done most of the work because Clémentine had found a pile of stale baguettes and had been slowly munching through them all. The tiny troughs that lined the edges of the tank had once again been filled with tasty insects so that the prisoners would be able to enjoy a last meal. As the frogs prepared to cross the narrow bridge, the cousins and Emile were on the road to collect Fred and his team. The following night the three of them would be feasting on raw frog and they could not wait.

Back at the tower, the journey across Fred's bridges had begun, although Hercule held back: "Mon dieu! You're not getting me to cross that flimsy thing! What do you think I am – an acrobat?" Ignoring him, Fred led the way, shouting encouragement over his shoulder to Gaubert who was at the front of a queue of nervous frogs.

"It's a breeze," yelled Fred. "Keep your eyes fixed ahead and you'll be fine. Once you get to the ground, head for the nearest barn in the cornfield and wait for me there." Frog after frog teetered along the walkway. They didn't go too fast for fear of slipping. But even so, some did fall off. A badger passing below was hit several times by falling amphibians and he was soon heard singing 'Fat Frogs Keep Falling On My Head' as he tucked into another unfortunate frog. Three frogs still to go: Hercule, Dimity and Lily. "Come on, les gars! We're almost there guys," urged Fred from the tree, where he felt his little heart overflowing with pride. "It's easy, you'll be great…Oh my word…"

"What is it, Fred?" asked Dimity.

"Hurry up! Just hurry up!"

"Why should we? We'll fall like the others if we rush and anyway I've told you nothing is going to make me cross that death trap!" retorted Hercule.

"It's the Bone Suckers! They're on their way; I can see their horrible yellow lorry in the distance. Get a move on but watch your step. Come on girls!"

"After me, I think," Hercule pushed his way past the other two and launched himself onto the first bridge, which shook precariously.

"Hercule, let the ladies go first," shouted Fred.

"It's too late," Dimity said, "he's already halfway. For goodness sake Hercule, slow down or you'll slip!"

"No, speed up," contradicted Lily, "the lorry's only three fields away!"

"What?" Hercule twisted around to hear better. It was the last word he ever spoke; his foot missed the wire and, with a howl, he toppled towards the ground.

"Lovely. C'est délicieux! Another tasty morsel!" The badger smiled as he caught Hercule and began to chew contentedly. "Who's next? This one tastes just a little bit bitter."

"Oh Hercule," Dimity was distraught.

"Out of the way, you," Lily almost knocked over the smaller frog as she bounded onto the twine.

"Oh well done, Lily," cheered Dimity as Lily joined Fred in the tree.

"Come on, Fred. Let's get out of here!" Lily was preparing to clamber down.

"Hang on a moment! Let's wait for Dimity! She's almost here." But things were not going terribly well for her.

I'm going to fall, thought Dimity as she was caught by a sudden gust of wind and wobbled dangerously.

"Come on, let go little frog, I'll catch you!" came the gruff voice of the badger from below. "With my teeth!" he chortled to himself.

Dimity gasped as she teetered on the wire. Fred's heart almost stopped as he watched. "Don't look down! Walk slowly towards the tree! Come on, Dimity, you can do it!"

"Hurry up! Stop being so feeble, Dim! I don't want to be caught," snapped Lily. Step by step Dimity edged onwards. "The van's coming! Hurry Fred, let's go," Lily started her descent.

Dimity saw a flash of yellow not far up the road and panicked, lost her balance and began to fall. Fred hurled himself along the bridge. "Here, grab my hand!" He stretched out and in a second had whisked the little frog back onto the bridge and then into the branches. The lorry screeched to a halt in the lay-by outside the tower, narrowly missing a fat, slightly disappointed badger. Out climbed the three Bone Suckers, two of whom then unloaded the tank and carted it into the tower. The third followed, a large piece of Brie held tightly in her hand. A minute later, Fred, Dimity and Lily heard angry voices coming from the top floor.

"What on Earth's happened? Somebody's nicked all the frogs!" shouted Emile. His sharp eyes spotted the broken window, through which he could just see the three frogs as they neared the bottom of the tree. "Downstairs! Now!" he screamed at Claude and Clémentine. "They're down there! Quick, dépêchez-vous, you fools, or there'll be no bone sucking tomorrow!"

Swearing madly, the men scrambled into the lift. "Come on Clem, get yourself in here, now!" Reaching the ground, Lily's eyes widened as the door of the tower was thrown open and the men rushed out with Clémentine breathing heavily in their wake. Sobbing fearfully Lily pushed past Dimity, only to trip on a root. "My ankle!"

"Here, Lily let me help you up," Dimity held out her hand.

"It's alright, I've got her. On you go, we'll meet you in the barn," said Fred. "We'll be right behind you."

Dimity got to the edge of the field, turned and watched in horror. Fred and a hobbling Lily couldn't see what was happening, but she could: "Watch out! Run!"

Claude had grabbed a net from the front of the lorry and was now racing towards them. With a deft swing, he swept them up and, still cursing loudly, returned to the lorry. He failed to see the lonely figure of a little frog weeping quietly as her hero was carried away.

Chapter 7
Late Night Diner: 'The Raw Frog'

As Fred and Lily found themselves in yet another tank in the back of the Bone Suckers' lorry, they certainly didn't feel up to their usual evening's entertainment of singing and dancing; Lily burst into tears. Although this alarmed Fred, he was becoming a tougher frog and could cope with limited amounts of water. There had, after all, been a great deal of weeping in the tower. Had Lily known that they were heading for 'The Raw Frog', a restaurant renowned for its fine food, she could well have put Fred's new-found tolerance of water to the test! Fortunately for them both, Lily and Fred were, for the time being, blissfully ignorant of the true horror ahead of them.

The lorry drew up outside the 'The Raw Frog' where a large group of Japanese tourists was getting off a coach and entering the infamous restaurant. While the tank was unloaded, some of the tourists gathered around, clicking their cameras and pointing at the frogs as they were transferred into a wooden box. Fred and Lily heard a creaking sound above them and noticed a signpost hanging outside the restaurant, swinging gently to and fro in the summer wind. Beneath the peeling paint they could still make out the picture of four frog's legs lined up beneath the body of a smiling, but legless, creature. They shuddered as reality dawned.

Inside the restaurant kitchen, the wooden box was placed in a larder but not before the waiters had all been summoned to admire the quantity of flesh on Fred and Lily's ample thighs. Eventually, the lights in the larder were switched off and the door was shut, locked and bolted; this was a meal that would not be allowed to escape.

The two little animals lay awake throughout the night, listening to the cockroaches scurrying and farting around the larder. Fred found himself thinking about home. "I wish I could say goodbye to everybody," he said wistfully.

"Don't waste time thinking about Dimity and that lot," spat Lily. "What are you going to do to get us out of here?"

"I didn't mean just them. I meant my family too. I was so horrible to my mother when I left and she was only trying to help. I wish I could see her just one more time to say sorry."

"And what good would that do? She'll have forgotten about you weeks ago. But my parents will be worried sick. I was about to get my big break."

"Really? Doing what?" Fred asked kindly.

"A film company was about to cast me as Veruca Salt," preened Lily.

"Veruca Salt?"

"The lead character in Charlie and the Chocolate Factory, obviously. The part was made for me! I always get the main part."

"Oh, I see." As Lily told endless tales of her brilliant childhood and early successes, Fred scanned her beautiful face but found himself thinking of little Dimity. He was remembering the many happy hours that they had spent chatting together; how she had listened to his worries; how he, in turn, had helped her overcome her shyness and insecurity.

"Of course, that was before I won my scholarship to dance school," Lily droned on.

Fred had enjoyed Dimity's openness and sensitivity and had loved relaxing in her company.

"My father's newspaper said I was the best they'd ever seen..."

Fred suddenly sat up abruptly; he and Lily needed to get out. He had to find Dimity.

Meanwhile, Claude, Clémentine and Emile were asleep in the grimy rooms of a nearby Bed and Breakfast. As Clémentine slept, a small stream of drool flowed out of the corner of her mouth; she was dreaming of raw frogs' legs.

Morning came. It was going to be a hot day but in the little larder at the back of the restaurant, it remained cool. Lily and Fred had succumbed to exhaustion in the early hours and little froggy snores escaped from Lily's pretty nose. The three Bone Suckers ate a breakfast of croissants, baguette and hot chocolate. They slurped their milky drinks, discussing their favourite subject: frog eating.

"Do you remember that frog last year who kept on trying to crawl away while you were blowing your nose?" Emile laughed, digging his elbow into Claude's ribs.

"Well, what about the time you smashed the plate when you were trying to stab that Norwegian frog with your fork? And then you cut yourself on a shard and bled all over the place!" Claude retaliated. "A right bloody mess."

"You still haven't got a clue how to eat a frog properly, Emile." Clémentine giggled. "And you," she turned to Claude, "O la Vache! You never get the legs off in one piece. I am the champion frog eater!"

"Rubbish!" said Claude angrily. "You're certainly the champion eater but when it comes to frogs, you're an amateur."

They argued as to who was the best at ripping off legs, who sucked the bones driest and, as they bickered, it slowly dawned on the three of them that there were only two frogs. The only thing that ever worried Clémentine was the thought of being denied food and so tempers began to fray even more and, as they stepped out into the street, a fight broke out. Claude bit his cousin's arm viciously, so she in turn punched him. Emile seized the cousins by the hair and knocked their heads together. Staggering a little and panting a lot, Clémentine called a halt to the battle. "That's enough, boys. I can't fight for long on an empty stomach, you know that."

"You're right; let's sort this out sensibly! Why don't we settle it with a game of boules? That won't be so exhausting for you. Whoever comes last goes hungry. Come on Clem, let's go and practise. See you outside the café at 12, Emile."

At midday, they met, as agreed and the competition began. Claude didn't take long to thrash his cousin who was all but blinded by a constant stream of sweat running off her brow. His eye was in and he beat Emile easily. "Okay, I'm going to have a drink. You two can fight it out. May the best player win!" He gave an almost imperceptible nod to his cousin, sat down at a table and beckoned the waiter. Ten minutes later Emile was on the verge of winning. Clémentine, who was looking very hot and bothered, only had one boule left. Up it flew before skidding to a halt on the gravel – it was close to the target ball, was it close enough? Emile began to rush forward with Clémentine not far behind him. "Wait!" Claude sprang up from his chair. "I'll do the measuring." He strode forward and knelt down, temporarily blocking the view of the two players. "So close! Tant pis! Hard luck, Emile, you lose by a whisker."

"Wait a moment, Claude, you've moved the balls around! There's no way Clem's ball ended up there!" growled Emile.

"Don't be such a bad loser. She won the game fair and square; take it on the chin, there's a good chap!"

"Cousins! Always cheating." Emile jumped into the lorry and, spinning its wheels furiously, sped into the distance in a cloud of dust. Clémentine licked her lips and patted her rumbling stomach.

"Good work, Clau. Thanks!"

In the kitchen of 'The Raw Frog', the chefs were cooking. The clatter of pots and pans woke Lily. "Fred, wake up!" She shook him roughly. "We're going to die! We're going to die! It's all over!" She gave a great sob and collapsed into the corner of the box.

"Stop it, Lily. Ecoute-moi! Listen! We're fast and strong, we can get out of this. Here's the plan."

"It's no good being fast and strong if you're dead, Mr Clever Clogs!"

"Oh Lily, be quiet and listen! The moment the cooks open this box, we've got to move faster than we've ever moved in our lives."

"Where to, for goodness sake?"

"Out of the box and then follow me. The instant we stop, we're dead. We want doors, windows, any way out! Keep jumping, keep moving!"

"And that's it? That's the great master plan, is it? Hercule was right about you! All talk! We're finished!"

"It's your choice, Lily." The sound of the larder door being unlocked interrupted them. "It's your choice," repeated Fred as he crouched, poised for action, his eyes fixed intently on the lid. Slowly Lily crouched next to him and waited, the adrenalin beginning to pump through her veins. They felt the box being lifted as it was carried into the noisy hubbub of the kitchen. Through the holes in the lid wafted the smell of freshly chopped garlic; they heard sizzling, as chips were dropped into hot oil and a babble of voices shouting orders and instructions. Footsteps hurried around them; Fred could make out the sound of swing doors swishing as waiters backed through them, plates stacked high. With a jolt, the box was placed on a work surface.

The head chef began to speak, "Attention! Take care with that, you fool! There's prized meat in there: the Bone Suckers have taken weeks producing it. Now sharpen those knives and get the plate ready!" Lily began to shake as she heard the screech of the knife against steel. The voice continued, "Watch this carefully and take note. You will be doing it next week. Take a plate and cover it with a layer of finely shredded lettuce, like so. Now that's easy but you need to be very careful as you take the frogs out of the box. I can do it with my eyes shut but that's because I'm an expert. Grasp the frog firmly around the middle with one hand – not too firmly or you'll break its ribs – with the other hand pick up one of these little mallets and give it a light tap on the skull just between the eyes."

"So that kills it, does it?" asked his assistant.

"No! Whatever you do you must not kill it. The Bone Suckers like fresh frog. The meat tastes sweeter like that. We stun them, the Bone Suckers kill them seconds before eating them. Finally, lay the frog on the plate and pop a sprig of fresh parsley in its mouth and cover it with one of the silver domes. Voilà!" Sweat broke out on Fred's forehead and he glanced at Lily.

"I'm fine, Fred. I'm ready, I'll follow you." Fred gave her arm a quick squeeze and they both crouched down again.

The chef continued, "The element of surprise is crucial." He placed his hand on the top of the box. "Three, two, one..."

"Go!" shouted Fred as the chef removed the lid with a flourish. The chef's jaw dropped open as the two frogs leapt past him, sending knives clattering to the floor.

"Oh I see! Thoroughly masterful, Chef!" tittered the assistant.

"Tais-toi! Stop laughing, you idiot and catch them! Everybody stop what you're doing and catch those frogs!" bawled the chef. Fred and Lily were, however, on the move.

"Vite! To the serving hatch, Lily," shouted Fred.

"Watch out for the soup," she yelled as they narrowly missed two steaming bowls of consommé. The bright light and heat of the hatch dazzled them briefly. "Where now, Fred? I can't see."

"Straight ahead," said Fred, squinting into the restaurant where he had spotted the back of a rather portly lady seated at a nearby table. "You take the left shoulder, I'll take the right." Off they sprang into the restaurant and onto the woman. She glanced to her left and then to her right, let out a piercing scream and jumped up, knocking the table over as she did so. The doors from the kitchen flew open as the red-faced chef burst into the restaurant brandishing a knife in each hand. Almost every guest was now on their feet, shouting and pointing everywhere. But in the far corner, two diners sat unmoved; Claude and Clémentine were in their own world and could think of only one thing: raw frogs' legs.

"Where are they?" cursed the chef.

"The chandelier, Fred, the chandelier," Lily pointed to the elaborate light fitting above them. Upwards they jumped, seizing onto the beautiful crystal arms of the chandelier just as the lady fainted and collapsed in a heap to the floor. The chef rushed towards where the frogs were swinging backwards and forwards on the light. The knives flashed evilly in his hands as he stretched towards the pair of them.

"I have you!" he hissed triumphantly, but just at that moment his right foot caught on the unconscious body and he was sent flying.

"Where now, Lily?" panted Fred.

"There's a window! That's where we need to go. How do we get there?" There was a whirl of people below them.

"One more swing and then onto the cheese trolley in front of it," answered Fred, "ready, steady, jump!"

Clémentine's reverie was suddenly interrupted by the sight of two figures she knew only too well sailing through the air towards a wedge of Brie. "Clau," she bellowed, "the frogs! They're escaping!" She stood up, too shocked to move any further. Her cousin snatched up a fork and launched himself with a roar towards the cheese trolley. He lunged at the frogs and a millisecond later the prongs were buried deep into the heart of...the cheese. Lily and Fred were now balanced on the far end of the trolley, which, as Claude crashed into it, sped towards the window.

"Two more jumps and we're out, Lily." Fred grinned. With a nonchalant hop, the two alighted onto the windowsill, turned to each other and smiled. He winked at her as they disappeared out through the window and into the bustle of the village below.

"Move, Fred! They'll be out in a moment; we're not safe yet!" Lily cried. "There, let's hide in that drain!" Swiftly they hopped to the gutter at the side of the road and took refuge in a dank, dark hole. Not a moment too soon, for seconds later Claude stormed out of the restaurant. Thirty seconds after that Clémentine emerged breathing heavily.

"Where's our supper?" She managed to gasp.

"Hey you, ugly! Did you see them?" barked Claude at an old lady walking her poodle. Puzzled, she fiddled with her hearing aid and shuffled on her way. "They can't be far," he shouted at Clémentine, "the fountain in the middle of the square! The wretches will be in there. Come on, run!" Into the road, he dashed, straight into the path of a van hurtling along at speed. He froze in horror as it screeched to a halt a few centimetres away from him, its horn blaring. Clémentine, who had sat down on a bench to recover from her exertions, watched events unfold with horror, saw an angry fist shaking at her cousin and then heard a woman's voice swearing furiously at him.

"Hey, Fred, jump onto the back of the van before it goes!" Lily sprang up, followed immediately by Fred. Meanwhile, Claude backed out of the way of the vehicle, while the driver revved the engine threateningly. As the van careered away the cousins saw the two frogs jumping up and down gleefully. Claude snarled in fury and tumbled towards where their lorry had been parked.

"Come on, follow me!"

"For heaven's sake, where is it?" Clémentine sighed, pushing herself wearily up from the bench.

"Emile took it," Claude held his head in his hands. The pair of them sank to their knees in despair. "What a disaster!"

On the van, Lily and Fred were still springing and somersaulting for joy. A pair of deep brown eyes was watching them intently in the rear view mirror. "Ça y est! We've done it," cheered Fred, "and all thanks to you, Lily. You were amazing!" He leaned towards her and planted a soft kiss on her forehead. "What a team!"

Chapter 8
Dimity in the Danger Zone

After Fred and Lily had been captured, Dimity didn't cry for very long, which would have surprised anyone she'd grown up with. Nobody had ever really had much faith in Dimity; she'd been incapable of making her mind up about anything, always needing to be with someone and lacking sparkle. Her friends...well, she didn't really have any. It wasn't that there was much wrong with her; it was just that she seemed a little bit dull. The other frogs only allowed her to play with them so that they could play tricks on her.

One day Dimity had been hanging around a group of her classmates who were chatting cheerfully together. "What are you talking about?" she asked.

"Nothing," replied a glamorous frog who then continued chattering away with her friends, "so then I said to him I'll meet you down by the river after lessons..."

"Are you going down to the river then?" piped up Dimity.

"No, I'm not," said the glamorous frog crossly.

"Dimity...Mind your own business!" the others groaned.

"But I tell you what Dimity," went on the glamorous frog with a cunning glance at her friends, "why don't you go down there for me and tell him I'm on my way?"

"Okay," beamed Dimity and off she went.

"She's going to have a long wait, I'm meeting him tomorrow!" sniggered the glamorous frog. "Come on everybody, let's go to the pond."

Dimity waited proudly down on the bank and then she waited proudly for a little bit more. The sun slowly began to sink and the shadows lengthened; Dimity's face grew longer as she realised that no one was going to come. Tears fell down her cheeks. She hopped off miserably and wandered along the river's edge in search of...to be honest, she wasn't sure what she was searching for. She just knew that there was no point in going to that school anymore. She didn't know what the future held but would take one day at a time. Things could only get better. Suddenly she was grabbed by her leg and dumped brutally into a bucket. Within hours, she found herself in the tower.

Strangely, Dimity was in fact quite happy there. She was not the only one who was confused and a little bit frightened. Whenever other frogs sank into depression, she would say the same thing to each one, "Just take one step at a time, one day at a time. Things can only get better." Most of the frogs were comforted by this friendly advice and so battled on, feeling a little bit happier. And then there was Fred. He was the first frog she talked to every morning; and every morning, without fail, he seemed optimistic. He was like a superhero. When he was not saving those stuck on a lower step, he would sit and talk to her for hours. He understood what it was like to be an outsider. He understood what it was like to be afraid. Dimity simply adored Fred and wished that he felt the same way about her. But every evening Dimity would watch as Fred took to the 'stage' to joke and sing and dance with Lily. Fred's face lit up as he performed and it was easy to see why, when you saw his partner. No one could deny that Lily was beautiful, talented and vivacious. There was no doubt that Fred and Lily made a handsome couple.

So when Claude's net had swept up Fred and Lily outside the tower, her idol was gone. Even though Fred and Lily would soon be dead, Dimity wished that she could have been in the net with Fred, instead of Lily. She knew, however, that sitting there crying would do nobody any good; her thoughts turned to the leaderless band of escaped frogs. They hadn't seen what had happened and were at that moment still waiting for Fred to tell them what to do next. She felt responsible for them and so, wiping away her tears, she hurried to the barn where they had been told to wait.

"Here comes Dimity, everyone!" shouted Cosette who was keeping watch. A loud cheer went up as the frogs rushed to the barn door.

"Where's Fred?" rang out a chorus of voices.

"What about Hercule? What have you done with him, then?" asked Gaubert.

Dimity hesitated, looked at the faces around her and steeled herself. "The badger got Hercule and the Bone Suckers caught Fred and Lily."

Cosette eventually broke the long silence that followed: "I'm frightened. I don't want to die," she whimpered.

"Well, I'm not going to die," declared Gaubert, beginning to move off. "Everybody for themselves!"

"Wait, Gaubert! We're safer together for the moment, don't you reckon? I think I can hear a stream over there. Why don't we head towards it and find somewhere to sleep for the night? Viens! Come on, Cosette, dry your eyes and let's get going." Dimity gently took control.

Shortly after they set off, the ground began to tremble and a loud rumbling sound could be heard not too far away. It was a combine harvester: a mean, chopping, slicing, hacking machine for harvesting crops. Dimity knew exactly what it was because in a picture book at school she'd seen one and she had imagined what it would sound and feel like. And...this trembling and rumbling was exactly what she had imagined it would feel and sound like! The frogs panicked and even Gaubert went white. Cosette took Dimity's hand. "I'm scared."

Dimity quickly cast her eyes about and saw nothing except a fluffy, white flash 20 metres away, which suddenly disappeared. Although she was no genius, Dimity knew that absolutely nothing except for ghosts vanishes into thin air. She also knew that ghosts only exist in dark, shady and haunted places and that a bright cornfield was none of these things. So the white flash, she concluded, must have gone somewhere. "Follow me," she ordered.

The noise of the combine harvester was growing louder by the second and the earth was quaking beneath the frogs' feet. Behind them the corn was swaying and then falling – their lives were in deadly peril. "This way! Vite! Quickly, down this hole." She gestured frantically at her friends to hurry and one by one they disappeared until only she was left. The thudding, cracking and crunching combine harvester was almost upon her when, with a swift bounce, Dimity too jumped down the rabbit hole

In the dark below, an angry rabbit with a fluffy, white tail was cursing at the stream of frogs who, without warning, had invaded his home. He ranted quite forcefully at the assembled group: "I happen to pay a huge rent for this hole and I'm jolly well not going to provide – at the drop of a hat, just like that, without so much as a how's your father – a home to any old frog who feels it appropriate to pop in left, right and centre unannounced and uninvited without so much as a please, thank you or sorry. I don't think so. Quel horreur!"

"Excusez-moi! I do apologise," said Dimity, "you must think we're terribly rude but it really was the only thing we could do. What a lovely home this is! It's simply delightful! If it's not too much trouble, you couldn't possibly show us around could you?" *A little tour,* she thought, *might calm down some of the more traumatised frogs.*

Flattered, Nigel the rabbit then spent hours showing everybody around his 'spacious, tasteful, glorious' accommodation. In truth, though, it was a little bit smelly as Nigel had been eating wild garlic leaves that morning. So when he finally waved goodbye to the frogs outside his backdoor, they each heaved a sigh of relief and gulped in a lungful of fresh air.

Dimity and the frogs emerged into another enormous field of un-harvested corn. The sound of flowing water was closer than it had been before and, in good spirits, they headed merrily in its direction, a strong wind cooling their brows. For half an hour they weaved in and out of the corn stalks until Gaubert, who was marching on ahead stopped abruptly. "Can you hear that? What's that noise?" They all listened.

"Fire! It's fire! I can smell the smoke," wheezed Cosette. She turned to Dimity, "What shall we do?" Dimity thought for a moment and then continued to head towards the crackling hiss. Dumbfounded, the frogs sat motionless. Towards the fire?

"Trust me," pleaded Dim.

Gaubert and two others shrugged their shoulders (they were French, after all) and fled in the opposite direction but the remainder hurried after her. The heat of the inferno was immense but on they hopped, their strong tower-muscled legs adding to their speed. As the first flickering tongue of fire was spotted so, finally, they noticed a deep ditch in the ground in front of them. It was narrow with a brook running along it. "Jump down!" begged Dimity. And jump down they did, just in the nick of time! Seconds later the wind-fuelled fire swept right over their heads and across the rest of the field. Poor Gaubert!

The survivors made their way down the ditch, exhausted by the emotion of the terrifying day. Before long, the brook emptied into the stream, whose gurgling they had heard from the barn so many hours earlier. The frogs climbed out onto its bank and trudged wearily along it for another hour before it swirled into a gorge with tiny, pebbly beaches on one side. "Right.

We'll stay here for the night," said Dimity, "find yourself somewhere under the bushes and try to get some sleep." Cosette snuggled up to her.

"Thank you for saving us, Dimity," she said sleepily. In the darkness, Dimity smiled thoughtfully.

As dawn broke, Dimity woke everybody and called a meeting. After much tedious discussion, the frogs elected to make the gorge their new base and urged Dimity to be their leader. Dimity would not accept their offer for she had another mission to fulfil; she was determined to find Fred's home. There she could inform his friends and his mother, Marie, of his brave deeds and his tragic death at the hands of the Bone Suckers. She walked over to Cosette. "I'm so sorry," she said gently, "I can't take you with me. It's too dangerous." Not daring to look back at the tiny frog, who was weeping quietly, Dimity left the gorge.

Chapter 9
Lady in Black

The driver of the van in which Fred and Lily had landed was a lady named Sabine de la Peur. She just happened to be a frog trainer. Throughout France, at that time, frogs were trained as acrobats and every four years, the Frog Circus Championship took place in Orléans. After the closing ceremony, a magnificent dinner, followed by a ball, was held for all trainers. The rules of the event were exceptionally strict and no frog was allowed to perform in two Championships: to prevent the law from being broken, all contestants were cooked and eaten at the dinner.

Sabine's life-long ambition was to prove that women were the equals of men even when it came to training frogs. No woman had ever won the gold medal. Sabine was a cruel but highly gifted trainer. When she had seen Fred and Lily celebrating their escape with a series of spectacular leaps in the back of her van, she had been elated. *Chouette! Finally, a little bit of luck* – she had smiled coldly to herself – *They're exactly what I need.* Once the van was some distance out of the village, she braked sharply and as it screeched to a halt, there was a sound of two thuds as the frogs slammed into the rear of the driver's cab. Fred and Lily were knocked out cold!

Sabine climbed out of the van, walked to the back and nodded to herself as she saw the unconscious frogs. "Perfect!" she said as she picked them up, returned to the driving seat and dropped them carefully into her bag before clipping it shut. She drove calmly back to the farm where she lived alone.

Most frog trainers were ugly, bad-tempered old men who cared little for their appearance. Sabine de la Peur was nothing like that. Her long glossy dark hair hung loosely around her shoulders framing her face, which, with its high cheekbones and deep brown eyes, was cruelly beautiful. She almost always wore black leather trousers and black cashmere polo-neck sweaters which suited her slender build and her mood.

She had inherited her good looks, as had her brothers, from her father, a successful and unusually handsome frog trainer himself. His two sons had spent their entire childhood learning his craft. Sabine had been a sweet little girl and had wanted nothing more than to join them in their discussions and activities. "Can I help?" she would ask eagerly.

"No! This is man's work. Go and hang out the washing for your mother," her father would growl. Slowly her nature changed; she grew bitter and eventually her smile, for so long angelic, lost its innocence. She became calculating and controlled although, when things went wrong, she suffered from violent outbursts of temper.

The two brothers went to university to study *Frog Coaching and Ethics* but Sabine was not allowed to follow them. Instead, she was sent away to a finishing school in Switzerland to learn how to sew and cook. How she detested this education! How she despised any meek girls and their lack of ambition. How furiously she shouted at her teachers! "I want to use my brain as well as my hands!"

"I hate cooking!"

"Why can't we study Mathematics?"

"What is the point of this wretched school? I'm an individual, not a robot!"

One day the headmistress called her to her study, "Sabine, Chérie," she chided, "your father would be ashamed of your behaviour. You must face it: your future is as a rich man's wife." Sabine's shoulders slumped but, on her face, she wore a look of steel as she left the room. The headmistress glanced down at the envelope that lay on her desk; in it, there was a cheque signed by Monsieur de la Peur for many thousands of francs. This girl would never be expelled.

Within weeks, Sabine had resolved to run away. On an icy November night, as the clock chimed 12, she wrapped herself in a roommate's fur coat, took what money she could find and sneaked out of the dormitory. Stealthily, she made her way down to the laundry room where she grabbed a handful of sheets. She tied them together to make a long rope, secured one end to the leg of an oak table and threw the other end out of the first-floor window. Sabine stood on the window sill and paused for a moment. "This is it, there's no going back now," she said out loud. She gritted her teeth and lowered herself slowly. The moment that her feet touched the frosted ground, she ran off like a black fox in the silver moonlight.

She settled in Paris and after many years had earned enough money to fulfil her ambition and become a frog trainer. She bought a farm not far from the city and paid the best frog coaches in the land to come and teach her. Day after day, week after week, month after month she improved her knowledge. After three long years, there was no more for her to learn. All she now required was a team of frogs worthy of her.

Sabine had already selected eight athletic frogs for training. The Championship rules stated that each team should consist of exactly ten frogs, no more, no less. Sabine had sought high and low for two more of the same calibre but had been unsuccessful until Fred and Lily somersaulted into her life.

Chapter 10
Crack of the Whip

Fred awoke with a thumping headache. Slowly his eyes focused and he registered that there was somebody lying next to him: "Lily" – he nudged her – "Lily, wake up!" The frog beside him stirred, "Ow! My head!" she groaned, "where am I? Arrête-toi! Stop pushing me!"

"Lily, it's Fred! I think the Bone Suckers have caught us again!"

"What! How on earth did that happen? Why did you let that happen? I thought you said you'd protect me?"

"There's no time for arguing. We're in some sort of barn; we'd better find a way out before somebody comes."

Then Lily seemed to remember herself. "Oh Fred, I'm sorry! Thank you so much. Thank you for rescuing me; you are wonderful! But would you check my head? It hurts. Is it bleeding? Is there a terrible gash? Am I going to be ugly for the rest of my life?"

"You could never be ugly, Lily, but it looks fine anyway." Fred replied, "We won't be, though, if we don't get out of here pretty quickly."

"There is no way out, I'm afraid," came a deep voice from nearby, "and it's not the Bone Suckers who have caught you but someone just as bad. Sabine de la Peur: she's a frog trainer and she's tough." Fred and Lily stared through the gloom in the direction from which the voice had come. "Mathilde, at your service." A large, muscular frog emerged out of the darkness and gave them each a powerful hug.

"Hi, I'm Frédéric and this is Lily."

"Pleased to meet you Ric, Lil. Welcome to the world of competition! We're being coached for the Frog Circus Championship and I reckon you're going to be the last two frogs on our team. Welcome!" Fred, sceptically, and Lily, like every frog, had both learned all about the Championship at school and they had heard tales of the greatest triumphs and the most marvellous feats of brilliance. But they also knew of the deadly fate that awaited all contestants. Lily gave a little shudder.

Several hours later the barn doors swung open and silhouetted against a bright sky was a figure swathed in black leather and cashmere; she was holding a whip in her right hand. "Up you get! To work! Tout de suite! NOW!" Sabine cracked the whip so that it hit the ground within centimetres of where Fred, Lily, Mathilde and seven other frogs had been snoozing. "Start warming up; leap frog races in teams of five."

So began weeks of training that seemed to last an eternity. But Lily was a swift learner and Fred possessed more athletic talent than any frog who had ever lived. They had soon mastered the tricks the other frogs already knew and, indeed, were beginning to outshine them. The fate that awaited them after the Championship was a distant threat and they lived for the moment, eager to avoid the wrath of de la Peur. It was hard work and Sabine was a merciless taskmaster.

One morning Jacomo, a small Italian frog and the weakest in the team, was standing in front of a flaming hoop. "I can't jump through it, it'll ruin my complexion," he said to the others.

Sabine saw him standing with his arms folded and flicked her whip so that it bit into the earth just behind him. "Jump or next time the whip will bite you and not the ground," she said in measured tones. Jacomo stayed stubbornly where he was.

"I'm too quick for the whip."

"Vas-y! Go on, Jaco," urged Fred, "you've got to do it or she'll kill you!" But the little fellow still did not move.

"I'll ruin your complexion and a whole lot more," Sabine's voice was still calm and yet threatening as she produced a box of matches, lit one and lowered the flickering flame slowly towards Jacomo's backside.

"Owwww! Take care, that's hot!" squawked Jacomo before sailing into the air and through the hoop.

"That is the punishment for cowardice," Sabine's velvet tones cut through the air, "anyone who wavers will face the same. This afternoon you will be springing over water tanks filled with hungry pikes. Judges are only impressed by skill, by courage and by daring. So you will all become skilful, courageous and bold, or there'll be trouble!" And so the training progressed day after day.

Later that month the frogs found themselves taken by their elegant coach into a room at the back of the barn. "Today," she began, "you will stop being mere gymnasts and will become acrobats."

Lily saw trapezes swinging to and fro high above her head. "Fred, I can't do that! Oh, my word! Is that blood on the floor?"

"Mais si! Of course, you can do it Lily," Fred spoke firmly, "don't you remember how we got out of 'The Raw Frog'? Just concentrate and you can do anything! We have to keep going; sooner or later a chance will come along for us to escape. You're an amazing gymnast. Come on, I know you can do anything!" Lily smiled gratefully and, surprisingly, a little shyly at Fred who gave her a friendly wink before turning to the other frogs to offer them encouragement.

Despite an accident or two, the frogs slowly grew in confidence as they swung from trapeze to trapeze. But it was always Jacomo who struggled with anything new and who often had to rely on the safety nets below. "I'm checking that they work," he claimed. The day of the Championship was drawing ever nearer and Sabine's patience was being tried by the little Italian's lack of talent.

"Listen, you wretched beast," roared Sabine one afternoon, as Jacomo plummeted downwards once more, "I had never used safety nets until you arrived. If a frog can't stay on the high wire or trapeze, it doesn't deserve to stay in my team. Luckily for you, I have nobody to replace you. But there are no safety nets at the Championship. If you fall, that is it. Curtains. Finished. Dead. Up you go again and this time try harder!"

"Shall I take a duster with me so I can do a bit of housework while I'm up there?" quipped Jacomo.

"Come on, Jacomo," pleaded Fred, "for your own sake! You can't come to any harm with the safety nets there and by the time we get to the Championship you'll be so good you won't need them. Just stretch, grab and hold."

"You're letting the rest of us down," Lily hissed out of the side of her mouth as she walked past him. "If I'm going to die on the plate of some frog trainer, I want to die with a gold medal pinned to my chest. I don't want a little weed like you ruining things." Then in a much louder voice, she went on, "Come on Jaco! Que tu es fort! You're terrific! Show us what you can do!"

"Good for you, Lil!" Fred gave her a friendly squeeze. Reluctantly Jacomo clambered up the ladder.

"Why can't I be given simple things to do? I'm very good at playing the triangle," he muttered loudly. Nevertheless, he reached the top of the ladder, seized hold of the swinging bar and leapt off the platform. "The things I do for others; I should be renamed St Jacomo!" He smiled as he swung. Three times he went back and forward before finally releasing his grip and sailing towards Mathilde on the opposite trapeze. "Go, go, Jaco! Go, go, Jaco!" shouted everybody from the ground below.

"Here, Jacomo, my hands! Take them!" Mathilde held them out to the little frog. He stretched, grabbed and held but only the tips of his fingers were in Mathilde's grip.

"I can't hold on," he shouted, "honestly, I can't hold on!" He slipped from her grasp and fell to the net below. "The safety nets are still working. I've just checked."

Sabine seized him furiously. "You useless fool! You're going to stop me from winning! What is the point of you?" She hurled him towards the barn door, his body smacking into it loudly.

"Aie! Agh! My leg!" yelped Jacomo. "I think it's broken! That wasn't a very nice thing to do!"

"Jaco!" shouted Fred and he rushed over to the door with almost all of the others. "It's alright, Jaco. You're fine. Everything's fine. Take it easy!"

"Fine? You call this fine? I'll be lucky if I ever waltz again!" Jacomo grinned weakly.

"Only nine frogs left," muttered Lily to herself, sitting casually on the safety net, "how can we win now?"

The same thought seemed to have occurred to Sabine who dashed over to the injured animal. She carefully picked him up and took him over to the First Aid box by the window. "You'll survive, little frog. You'll recover," her words came out almost gently as she attached a splint to his injured leg, "you've got to."

"Pourquoi? Why?" asked Jacomo. "So I can fall down again? Frogs aren't meant to fly; I want to be a florist not a stupid acrobat!"

The very next day a large envelope containing the programme for the tournament dropped through Sabine's letterbox. She ripped it open and flicked hurriedly through its pages: her team would be the final entry to perform and they would come immediately after the team of…Luc and Jean Paul de la Peur – her brothers! How could she beat them? Her team had to leave for the Championship in two days but she only had nine fit frogs!

Chapter 11
Tenth Man Down

Two days later, on a misty morning, Sabine loaded the frogs into a large tank in the back of her van and placed Jacomo on a soft cushion to keep him as comfortable as possible. His groans suggested that he was nevertheless still in pain. "It's lucky I have such a high pain threshold. Me, I suffer in silence. Owwwwww!" Sabine knew that, in all probability, she had to find another frog.

"Keep the noise down, Jacomo, would you? I'm trying to rest. Aren't you being just the slightest bit feeble, not to mention selfish?" Lily scolded.

"I'm so sorry, Lily, how thoughtless of me! You're right, it must be because you're tired that you're not looking your best; I'll just try and die quietly." Lily turned away from him and hopped over to where Fred was talking seriously to the rest of the frogs.

"Listen, once we've left the farm, we might just get the chance to escape. I want you to be alert and ready to run at all times, do you understand?"

"Bien sûr! Of course. You give the word," replied Mathilde, "and we'll follow you. But what about Jacomo?"

"I'll carry him on my back if the worst comes to the worst," Fred smiled at Mathilde.

That idiotic Italian will wreck our chances, thought Lily but she kept her views to herself and, catching Fred's eye, gave him a saccharine smile.

Back inside, Sabine was packing meticulously. Into her smartest suitcase, she folded her lucky, black velvet coat and her favourite, black cashmere polo-neck sweater. She walked out of the front door and whistled into the swirling mist for her dog. "Viens! Here, now! Come here now!" She turned to her chef who was emerging from the dining room with a plate on which sat her untouched breakfast of smoked salmon. "Where has that wretched animal disappeared to?"

"I put him outside at six o'clock, as usual, Madame," he answered.

"There is no time to spare; I can't wait or we'll miss our reservation for the morning practice session in the main arena," Sabine spoke angrily, "don't feed him while I'm away. That'll teach him a lesson." She strode outside, jumped into the van, slammed the door and sped off down the drive. Suddenly, as if from nowhere, a ball of fur flew through her open window and landed, panting, on the passenger seat next to her. "Cutting it a bit fine, aren't you?" she gave the dog a quick pat.

As the sun burnt off the mist, the van hurtled along the rural lanes of France. Sabine's mind was elsewhere. "How can I change the act so a frog with a damaged leg can still perform?" she asked herself. It was rare for Sabine to feel regret for her actions, but even she was beginning to wish that she hadn't lost her temper quite so violently. Whatever possibilities sprang into her mind, she knew that the alterations would drastically weaken her team's chances of success. Her concentration began to drift until, twenty kilometres into the journey, her keen eyes suddenly spotted a tiny creature hopping along the country road, way off in the distance. It couldn't be a frog because its leaps were far too high for such a little creature. But it was definitely much too small for a rabbit or a hare. Its slightly peculiar motion reminded Sabine of Fred and Lily, whose powerful back legs still amazed her. Surely it couldn't be another frog like them?

With desperate hope etched on her face, Sabine drove like a woman possessed up the lane and, just as she overtook the little animal, she leant out of her window and scooped it up. Giving an uncharacteristic whoop of delight, Sabine stamped on the brakes and the van ground to a halt. In her hand, she held a small, plain frog with large eyes and huge thighs. The little frog sat in the palm of Sabine's hand and stared up at her. Sabine stepped out of the van and walked around to the back where she carefully opened the lid of the tank just wide enough for her to place the tenth frog on the floor and to snatch Jacomo from his cushion. "Oh hello again, quelle surprise! What can I do for you?" he asked.

"Farewell, you useless creature!" She laughed as she threw the Italian into the hedge at the side of the road.

The frogs, who remained behind, could just make out Jacomo shouting, "There goes my other back leg – that's the end of my tap-dancing career! Been nice knowing you all!" before the van set off again.

The tenth frog blinked in the darkness of the tank and slowly she made out the familiar shape of a face she knew. "Fred?"

"Dimity?" came his shocked reply.

"Dimity!" exclaimed Lily. In the semi-darkness, nobody could see her scowl.

Chapter 12
The Championship

Dimity and Fred had hugged and hugged when they had been reunited in the tank, whilst Lily, after her private scowl, had given a small nod of acknowledgement and a tight smile. Once they had caught up with each other's adventures, attention naturally turned to the next challenge. Within an hour of arriving at the Frog Circus Championship, the team found themselves on a platform inside the great arena.

Dimity stared around her and gasped in a mixture of awe and confusion, "Fred," she asked, "why's everything made of blue rubber?"

Fred shrugged his shoulders. "I've no idea. Anyone?"

Mathilde spoke up confidently. "The stadium isn't just used for the Frog Circus Championship, it also hosts the Trout Show-Jumping Tournament."

"Oh don't be ridiculous, sois sérieux!" interrupted Lily. "Whoever heard of trout doing show-jumping? How gullible are you Mathilde?"

"I'm sorry but it's true," continued the big frog, "that's why the middle of the stadium is like a swimming pool. And look in the corners! Those holes drain away the water once the event's over. I met a trout years ago who'd come 15th. He told me all about this place."

"15th! What a loser!" scoffed Lily. "Well Ms Know-All, I suppose you can tell us what this platform's for then?"

"So when we frogs perform our acts we can be seen by everybody, silly!"

"Who are you calling silly? How dare you!" Lily stared furiously at Mathilde.

"Lil, be quiet for a moment and listen!" Fred gave a smile.

"Thanks Ric! Look! Feel the floor: it's made of oak and it's springy to help us bounce. Our trampolines will be moved up here too."

"Where do the judges sit? And how can they see exactly what we're doing?" asked Dimity.

"Can you see those five gigantic gold plated stools over there?"

"On the side of the stadium without any seating?"

"Yes, that's where they sit. And they can watch everything on those huge screens hanging down from the ceiling. There are even loudspeakers in the corners to play any music that the trainers want to use for the acts."

"What's on the flashy balcony above the stools, Mathilde?" Fred's eyes gazed upwards.

Mathilde gave a half laugh. "A three star Michelin Restaurant. All the teams get cooked and eaten up there after the show, I'm afraid. Usually fried in garlic!"

"Fred!" screeched Lily. "Fred, why have you brought me here?"

"Fred, will that happen to us?" Dimity asked quietly.

"Not to us, not to us! We'll be alright, I promise." Fred whispered quietly to his friends.

The next couple of days saw a frantic schedule being undertaken by Sabine's squad. There was a Championship to be won and Dimity had much to learn. She watched the others carefully and then practised and practised and practised with intense determination. Despite frequent wobbles, she soon knew what she was doing. Almost.

The great day finally arrived and Sabine awoke from a restless sleep to the sound of a heavy downpour and the ceaseless drumming of rain against the window panes. She let the dog out and dressed carefully in cashmere sweater and leather trousers before putting on her black velvet coat, lined with green silk, to which she pinned a silver brooch of a leaping frog. She nibbled nervously at a corner of a croissant but couldn't finish it. Fred, Lily, Dimity and their fellow performers were equally tense as they waited.

If we could just win, it'd show I'm worth something, Fred thought, *I must've been such a disappointment to Mum; honestly, a frog who's scared of water! A gold medal and I could go home and show it to her and then, just maybe, she'd be proud of me. Anyway, I certainly don't want to be eaten by de la Peur.* He carefully studied the design of the arena until he worked out a plan. As the frogs in Sabine's team waited, he started to explain, "We've got to get out tonight and I think, if everything goes our way, we can manage it."

"Well, your idea better work because I haven't done all this training so that I can end up in that woman's stomach," Lily muttered to herself.

“Fred helped us beat the Bone Suckers in the tower, Lily,” said Dimity, who had overheard, “and he’ll save us again now!”

“Pas moi! He didn’t get me away! You were fine, skipping off into the cornfield without a thought for me but I ended up in a restaurant,” snapped Lily.

“But you’re here now and that’s because of Fred! Anyway, let’s be quiet and listen to him.” Dimity put an arm around her teammate who shrugged it off angrily before nestling up to Fred who was still speaking.

Five minutes later Fred finished. “Everyone clear then? Now let’s win the title and get out of here!”

Dimity gazed up at her hero whilst Lily looked deep into his eyes. “Oh Fred, you’ll keep me safe, won’t you?” she simpered.

“Of course, I will, Lil!” he answered. She smiled prettily. “I’ll keep you all safe,” Fred promised.

Historians who have written about the Frog Circus Championship of that year are agreed that the standard was never higher. The first four teams came, in order, from: Paris, Strasbourg, Rouen and Marseilles. The audience was thrilled by the brilliance of the opening act; shocked by the daring of the second; they roared their approval of the third; and gasped in fear as they watched the fourth. Frogs bounced, flew, spiralled and swung.

Then the drums rolled announcing the arrival of the fifth team. Luc and Jean Paul de la Peur’s frogs marched briskly across the entire length of the arena, up the ladders and onto the stage. They were magnificent. Tightropes were crossed swiftly with one frog on the shoulders of another. One little chap dived from four metres into a bowl of water; not a single drop splashed onto the wooden floor. To complete the show, all ten frogs somersaulted across the stage with military precision to the sound of a ten-gun salute. The spectators erupted in applause. Even Sabine clapped reluctantly. *How on earth can my frogs beat that?* she wondered sadly.

The moment of truth arrived for Sabine de la Peur and her team. A trampoline was placed in each corner of the stage. Then the lights dimmed, the crowd fell silent and a lone flute began to play softly. One by one the trampolines were illuminated by spotlights as frogs began to bounce, twist and spin. Gradually clarinets, oboes and bassoons; violins, cellos and violas; trumpets, horns and tubas joined the flute, the swelling of the music matching the growing daring of the performers. The frogs criss-crossed through flaming hoops of fire, flying smoothly past each other, almost – but never quite – colliding.

Next, they built a pyramid of frogs with Fred alone at the top. As cheers rang out, Fred flipped to the floor and two of his teammates landed, one on each of his shoulders. Three more leapt onto them and the final four completed the reversal of the pyramid. Fred's strength defied belief.

Now it was time for the trapeze. Fred and Mathilde held on to opposite swings and threw Lily between them as she completed increasing numbers of elegant somersaults. Three was breathtaking, four was incredible, five was the world record and as for six – not even the brilliant Lily would try six! Then Dimity joined in and copied Lily's acrobatics as they were thrown past each other from trapeze to trapeze. Finally, a chain of four frogs hung on to each swing with Lily and Dimity being tossed between the two chains with apparent ease!

As the act neared the end, Dimity flew for the final time towards the opposite trapeze. She was close to exhaustion and didn't time her jump perfectly. Fred, who was now, in the position of a catcher only caught one leg. *Zut! I knew that tenth frog wasn't up to it,* thought Sabine who was watching intensely, why didn't she put both her front legs out properly? She held her breath, gripping the arms of her seat so tightly that her knuckles went white.

Dimity meanwhile felt herself beginning to slip from Fred's grasp. Terrified, she stared up into his eyes and as she did so, glorious memories of the tower flooded through her mind, each one of Fred reaching down to her from the top of a step and pulling her up alongside him with a big grin.

"Pour moi! Do it for me, Dim," he whispered firmly, willing her to reach out before the trapeze swung him away. The urgency of his words and the concern on his face spurred her on to find one last ounce of strength. She stretched up and Fred seized her second leg firmly, just in the nick of time. "Got you, little Dimity, got you!"

"Oh Fred, thank you!" beamed Dimity. In her seat, Sabine relaxed, allowing herself the smallest of smiles, whilst the crowd stood and cheered.

As they finished the act, Sabine felt a warm glow of pride as she absentmindedly patted her silver frog brooch. The five judges climbed down from their stools and conferred for some time. A buzz of anticipation filled the arena. Who had won? Eventually the head judge, a warty, ancient man who smelled strongly of feet, hobbled up onto the restaurant balcony and slowly began to announce the results.

"In third place, Arnoux – Thierry!" The team from Marseilles had won bronze. "The runner-up is…" The man paused to itch an unpleasant scabby wart on the side of his neck "de la Peur…" (Sabine's hopes soared. She had won silver!) '…Luc and Jean Paul!'

Sabine's heart almost stopped. "Have I won gold? Oh, my word! No, of course, I haven't! I've come last! Those hundreds of hours of training have been wasted and all because of that tenth frog. Wait till I get my hands on her! Quel désastre! Yes, this is a disaster; a total humiliation. I'm going to have to disappear into obscurity forever. Those Parisians have won. I've failed."

Sabine was so caught up in herself that she almost missed the final announcement. "And the winner of this year's Championship is," Sabine scowled jealously at the smug trainer from the capital city, who was smiling confidently as he stood up and began to make his way over to the balcony steps, "de la Peur – Sabine!" The crowd leapt to their feet, cheering wildly. As Fred's eyes met Dimity's, Lily swooned dramatically and he had to turn away to catch her. Meanwhile, Mathilde enveloped Dimity in a crushing embrace. Sabine gave an almost bashful smile and the entire audience sighed at her gracious beauty. She glided up onto the balcony, past the Parisian trainer and her two astounded brothers, before charmingly accepting her prize of a solid silver tank. A de la Peur had done it! A female de la Peur!

It was traditional for the winning team to repeat their final performance before they were cooked and Fred and his friends were soon gathered again on the trapeze. They were full of excitement and hope. As their act neared completion, they swung ever more strongly and, over the speakers, Sabine – as serene as ever – announced in a divinely smooth voice, "The previously impossible sixth somersault will now to be attempted by my team. Two frogs will simultaneously perform the trick with both being caught by the opposite chain of four frogs!" The crowd murmured and then grew quiet.

Ten times the trapezes swung, each time a little higher and then – catastrophe! At the very moment that Fred lost his grip on Dimity, Mathilde lost hers on Lily and suddenly ten frogs were flying in all directions. Sabine screamed and shut her eyes, the crowd screamed and shut their eyes and the judges screamed and shut their eyes; the only thing they were all still aware of was the over-powering smell of the chief judge's feet. The frogs, meanwhile, landed gracefully and miraculously uninjured on the rubber floor and hopped silently towards whichever drain was the closest to them and disappeared.

"Allons! Move! Run! Quickly!" urged Fred. The judges opened their eyes, the crowd opened their eyes and Sabine opened her eyes. The smell had not vanished but the frogs had!

Chapter 13
Crash!

The Orléans Stadium was a stone's throw from the outskirts of the city. When it was being built, the locals who objected to its construction had, led by a vicious old lady, hurled stones from their gardens at the poor innocent builders. In one direction, there lay the somewhat grim suburbs, while, to the other, was dirty, scrubby undergrowth. Beyond the undergrowth was a dark and brooding forest (said to be haunted) through which wound a sluggish stream. Once Fred and his friends had fled down the drains, they followed the pipes which looped to the back of the stadium. The damp reminded them of their homes and made them more determined than ever to get out.

"Which way now?"

"It's so dark. We're all going to die!"

"No we won't, Fred told us to meet behind the stadium."

"Do we take this turning?"

"No, I think that will go back to the stadium. Oh sorry, Lily, was that your foot?"

"Watch where you're going, Dimity, I bruise terribly. Fred likes me to be at my best at all times."

"I can see light and look, there are some of the others ahead of us!"

"Hey, Fred! Me voilà! Here I am. I'm safe, I've done it." Lily raced ahead and flung herself into Fred's arms.

"Well, done Lily!" Fred gave her a kiss on her forehead. "Where are Dimity and the others?"

"Here, Fred, we're all here."

The frogs emerged triumphantly from a narrow tunnel. The sky was black and angry and it was pouring with rain. "Let's make for that wood before she comes after us," said Fred.

Sabine was indeed hot on their trail. When she had opened her eyes and had seen no sign of the frogs, she knew at once that they had escaped. She scanned the arena below, rapidly spotting the drains and guessing correctly where her team had gone. She strode swiftly to the staircase, which led down from the balcony to the ground floor. Down the steps Sabine swept, her mind working out in a trice what to do. She reached the entrance to the Stadium and took five paces out into the storm. Soon rain was dripping off her dark hair as lightning flashed overhead and thunder rumbled.

She whistled loudly and two minutes later a snuffling bundle of dog stood panting at her side. Crash, the Froghound, was the result of years of expert breeding. He was like a scruffy Bearded Collie but there was one important difference. Crash had two particularly long teeth in the same position that vampires have their particularly long teeth. When sniffing out frogs, he would wedge them between these teeth and, with a flick of his strong neck, would send the frogs hurtling up, along and then down into a box that was strapped to his back. The lid to this box consisted of two hinged pieces of wood, which could swing inwards but not outwards, so that Crash could continue to hunt without fear of captured frogs escaping.

Sabine inspected her faithful hound sternly and produced from a pocket one of the whips that she had used for training the frogs. She held it to Crash's nose and he took in the scent. "Seek and deliver!" She purred in soft, honey-like tones. With a wag of his tail and an excited yelp, Crash turned around in a series of tight circles. "I said 'Seek and deliver', you fool!" cursed de la Peur and gave the frog hound a kick. Crash rushed off towards the back of the stadium where he searched around for a few moments before releasing a bloodthirsty howl and disappearing into the trees.

Fred, Lily, Dimity, Mathilde and the rest of the frogs had gathered underneath an old oak tree just inside the forest. One of the others, Alain, now spoke, "Hey, this is a pretty good way to celebrate my birthday! A gold medal and then freedom! It's my best birthday ever!"

Lily burst into song. "Happy Birthday to you, Happy Birthday to you," she warbled.

"Hadn't we better get a move on?" Dimity whispered to Fred who nodded.

"Come on everyone! Time to go," he said.

"What about 'The Bumps'?" asked Alain, "I want 'The Bumps'. It's not a real birthday without 'The Bumps'!"

"Oh, do be quiet or I'll give you a bump on the rump," interrupted Lily impatiently.

The rain was beating down ever more heavily and all this water was making Fred frightened and keen to be on his way and in the dry. "We'll follow the track beside the stream. It's bound to lead to a pond!"

"Good idea, Fred," chirped Dimity.

"Tu penses! Not exactly Einstein at work," Lily grumbled to herself.

As they tripped merrily along they noticed, one by one, just how dark, brooding and possibly haunted the forest was. So when they heard a blood-curdling howl not far behind them, they feared the worst. "What's that sound?" whimpered Alain. "It must be a ghost and I don't like ghosts. And this one sounds the scariest kind. This is the worst birthday I've ever had. I'd rather be eaten by Sabine than killed by a ghost," he snivelled.

"It'll be alright…" Fred's voice trailed away as he saw, coming through the undergrowth, an awful and solid sight. This was no phantom; it was a frog hound and it was a mere 200 metres behind them and although the undergrowth was dense, it wasn't dense enough to deter Crash.

Suddenly the dog raised his head, saw the frogs, howled again and, in an instant, was leaping towards them. Nine frogs jumped into the stream. "Come on, Fred," shouted Dimity but he stood on the bank quivering with fear.

"I can't, I just can't!" he moaned to himself as two extra-long teeth belonging to Crash headed towards him.

With virtually no warning at all, a flash flood came rushing down the stream, picking up everything in its path and sweeping it away. As Crash's teeth descended towards Fred, a large wave swept the frog off his feet into the centre of the raging torrent. Even Crash himself was briefly knocked over by its force.

Fred found he was hurtling downstream alarmingly fast and was up to his neck in horrible, swirling, foaming water. He was close to outright panic when alongside him he noticed something. *If I could just reach that,* he thought desperately, stretching out one leg towards a long piece of bark. He grasped the side of it and heaved himself onto it. The bark was concave, forming a perfect kayak. It was ideally shaped to travel rapidly through the water and soon Fred was catching up with the others and, briefly overcoming his terror, he gave nine smart flicks of a leg and nine frogs, who had been struggling in the power of the flood, joined him on board. Crash had not, however, given up and was bounding after them before they had had a chance to thank Fred. A branch had fallen across the stream and the kayak full of frogs rushed underneath it at full tilt. There was no room for Crash to do the same and he smacked straight into it. Both vampire teeth were knocked out of the poor dog's mouth and vanished beneath the foaming water. He was now like a gun without bullets – useless – and he knew it. Tail between his legs he loped back towards the Stadium where Sabine, scarcely visible against the brooding sky, still stood at the entrance in the teeming rain.

The exhausted dog came up to her side, his tail between his legs and his mouth tightly shut. She peered into the box on his back. "Rien? Nothing?" she barked. "Open your mouth!" The dog reluctantly moved his bleeding lips apart revealing two gaps where there should not have been gaps.

A look of anger passed across Sabine's face but it was slowly replaced by a smile, a warm smile that she had not worn since she was a young girl. "Well, Crash, it seems that I won't be eating frog tonight after all. But do you know something?" she knelt down beside her dog and patted him lovingly. "N'importe! I don't really care. I've won the Championship; I've done it and shown everybody what I can do. No more frog training for me! We'll do something more worthwhile with our lives. But first of all, let's go home and in the morning we'll find a dog dentist for your poor old teeth. Good boy."

Crash looked adoringly up at his mistress and wagged his tail. Together they walked into the night.

Chapter 14
The Rapids

As Sabine drove home, happily planning her future, Fred and his gallant band of frogs were in the middle of a stream that had turned into a terrifying log flume. The piece of bark that they were using as a kayak was spinning about wildly in the water and, although it was still afloat, it was out of control. Frogs may generally be at home in the water, but such was the force of the flood that to fall overboard would soon have killed them.

There was pandemonium. "Mathilde, get to your own side of the boat! You're going to tip us all into the water," shrieked Lily.

"What kind of birthday do you call this?" whined Alain.

"Watch out we're about to hit that log; hold on tight!" gasped Dimity.

"I'm going to be sick – it's so rough," Alain was really very unhappy.

"Steady, everybody, steady," Fred's voice shook slightly.

The bark whooshed around a bend in the stream. "What on earth is that noise?" Lily sounded genuinely scared.

"Rapids! Or a waterfall!" guessed Dimity.

"We're doomed – and on my birthday!"

"The boat's all over the place; we've got to keep it straight," Even Mathilde was worried. There was no way that they would be able to negotiate rapids as they had no method of steering the boat. Fred, despite the horror of being surrounded by water, was racking his brains for yet another plan. He could not produce one. Had he and his friends escaped from de la Peur only to be killed tragically in the turbulent water? Fred glanced miserably and fearfully into the stream that he was sure would soon claim his life.

He caught his breath and leapt to the other side of the bark. "What are you doing, you idiot! You're making the boat wobble," shouted Lily as Fred, fighting his fear, stretched a hand out into the torrent.

"Oh Lily, do get out of his way – please!" Dimity somehow remained polite, despite the urgency of the situation.

"Hold on to my arm, Mathilde," shouted Fred as he leant way out over the edge of the vessel.

"Got it!" Mathilde pulled him back to safety. Fred had snatched a piece of wood out of the stream and now hurried to the back of the boat where he plunged the stick into the water, using it as a rudder to steer. The kayak – for that was what it had become – straightened and, as it rushed towards the top of the rapids, Fred succeeded in positioning it more or less perfectly. Down the boat rushed, spray everywhere. The bark tilted, bucked and shied but Fred kept it on course.

Then, all of a sudden, Lily found herself knocked over the side of the boat by a huge wave. As her head began to disappear beneath the water, she felt herself being grabbed and pulled back up. "I've got you, it's okay," A huge smile of relief shone on Dimity's face as she heaved Lily back on board. But her smile vanished almost immediately as she herself was sent flying overboard by a second wave. Dimity managed to seize the side of the boat. "The current's too strong, I can't hold on." She turned her head pleadingly to Lily and their eyes met. "Lily, au secours! Help me!" Lily held Dimity's gaze for a split second before she began to faint slowly and gracefully in shock.

"Hors du chemin! Out of the way!" With a cry of horror, Mathilde pushed the swooning Lily aside and snatched Dimity into her arms, yanking her back on board. Lily's eyes fluttered open slowly and alighted on Fred, but he hadn't seen any of the drama; he was too busy steering. Nor did he see Mathilde trip and lose her balance…"Help!" Dimity tried desperately to catch her, but it was no good. Mathilde's head hit the side of the boat and she dropped, unconscious, into the water. There was nothing Dimity could do. Mathilde was lost forever beneath the seething foam.

"Fred, how awful!" Dimity turned to him in horror. "I couldn't save her; it happened too fast."

"Poor Mathilde! But I couldn't do anything either. I had to keep steering us. If I hadn't kept us in the middle of the current, we'd all have died."

"Oh for goodness sake, will you concentrate!" Lily's irritated cry rang out.

Fred and Dimity's eyes locked for a few seconds before he gritted his teeth and grimly turned his concentration back to the rapids.

The stream eventually widened into a broad and smoothly flowing little river – the frogs were safe at last. Lily made her way to the back of the boat and gave Fred a big kiss. "Oh my Fred, you're wonderful! You're my hero." He blushed.

"But we lost Mathilde," Fred said with a catch in his voice.

"I know; it's so sad." Lily stroked his arm for a few minutes and then rejoined the other frogs. Soon she began to sing a lament for Mathilde.

"Oh when water into the boat it spilled,
We all relied on good old Mathilde,
It's such a pity she's now been killed!"

Chapter 15
Bitten!

Fred sat slumped by the tiller thinking sadly about life and death. As adventure had followed adventure, he'd become a much wiser frog and he now saw how fortunate he had been to have a loving mother like Marie. *If only I could see her again, I'd tell her about everything that's happened; I'd introduce her to everyone…I'd say sorry,* he thought, *Oh I wish I were at home!* He simply had to find his way back to his family but first he needed to get his feet on dry land. "Hard astern!" He had seen a muddy bank on which they could pull up. Fred hopped ashore with a sigh of relief and slumped under a tree. Slowly the others followed and collapsed around him. They sat in silence for a while.

"Thank you, Fred. You've saved us again," said Dimity standing up and moving towards him.

"Except for Mathilde," whispered Lily in her ear as she leapt up and pushed Dimity aside. "What's the plan now Fred, darling?"

Fred ignored Lily. "I need to go home, I want to see my family. I want to see my mother," he said, staring into the distance. "In the morning, I'm leaving. You can come with me if you want. I'd like you to meet her." He closed his eyes. "But now we need to rest." They all settled down except Lily who sat a little way apart contemplating Fred.

The sound of birdsong and the warmth of the sun on their faces woke them. For the first time in months, they were free. After breakfast, Fred gathered them together. "It's time for me to go. Is anyone coming with me?" He smiled at them.

Dimity smiled back and walked slowly towards him; Lily rushed past her. "Of course, I'm coming with you, Fred. I can't wait to meet your family."

"Moi aussi! You can count on me, too," chipped in Alain.

"That's four including me. Anyone else?" asked Fred. "It's not going to be easy."

The other frogs gathered together and spoke for several minutes before explaining apologetically to Fred that they were tired; that they had had enough of adventures and that they thought that the place where they had stopped would make a perfect home. Then they all hugged Fred, Alain and the girls and there were a lot of tears and promises to keep in touch.

"Bon! Right, off we go. Let's pick up the boat," said Fred eventually.

"Really? What on earth do we need it for?" Lily raised her eyebrows.

"You just never know," Fred was thinking of the rivers, streams and ponds and all the water that might lie ahead; he wasn't taking any chances.

"It'll be so hard carrying it. It's a waste of time."

"Lily, we're taking it and that's final."

They lifted the bark onto their heads and set off. Several hours later they halted in a small glade in a wood to rest. Fred couldn't relax and paced up and down wondering whether they were going in the right direction. He didn't notice a snake slithering towards him out of a pile of rotting logs.

Dimity did notice. "Oh my goodness, Fred! Don't turn around; keep calm and just walk slowly towards me. There's a snake just behind you."

Lily noticed too. "Help! I don't want to die!" She turned and fled.

As Lily ran for safety, she passed Alain who was moving with grim determination in the opposite direction, past Dimity and just as the snake was about to strike at Fred, Alain leapt in front of it. "Mais non! No, you don't!"

The others watched in horror as the snake sunk its fangs into the little frog, who shuddered as the venom coursed through his veins; then he was still. The snake swallowed Alain's lifeless body whole and slid blithely into the undergrowth.

Fred looked aghast at Dimity as Lily emerged sheepishly from behind a clump of flowering hyssop. "Alain! Was that really Alain?" cried Fred. "I never realised he was so brave. And now that I do, it's too late because he's dead and it's all my fault. He was a true friend, a hero! How many more friends am I going to lose? How can I forgive myself? No more birthdays, Alain my friend, no more birthdays. What is the point of going on? I just keep getting things wrong. I'm useless."

"Alain worshipped you, Fred. He didn't think you were useless. He learned from you; he'd be happy that he saved you. If you don't make it home now, he'll have wasted his life. You owe it to Alain to go on," Dimity spoke in a voice close to breaking.

In silence, the three frogs picked up the kayak and continued on their way.

Chapter 16
Homeward Bound

By mid-afternoon, they had arrived at a small crossroads in the heart of a wood. A white signpost pointed in various directions: Vierzon, Orléans and Fontainebleau. "Which way, Fred?" asked Dimity.

"Fontainebleau!" hooted Fred. "Fontainebleau's really close to home; we learned about it in Geography at school."

"But what's the number next to it? 83 kilometres," groaned Lily "We'll never be able to hop all that way."

"Sois sage! Don't be silly, Lily, Fred will think of something," Dimity smiled.

"Silly? Me silly? Who couldn't jump up the steps in the tower without help? Who got caught so easily by Sabine? Don't you dare call me silly when you're the one who's always getting things wrong!"

"Stop it you two, I'm trying to think!" interrupted Fred. Lily turned her back to Fred with her nose in the air while Dimity, head hanging, wandered unhappily a few metres down the road to Fontainebleau. Fred sat down and put his brain into gear.

A minute later Dimity hopped up excitedly. "Hey, you two. There's a car parked around the corner; why don't we try and hitch a lift in it?"

"And get spotted, captured and eaten? Oh brilliant, Dimity!" snorted Lily.

"Hang on," said Fred, "I think you could be on to something there, Dim! Show me where it is." The vehicle had no rear bumper but unobserved and lying asleep on the front bumper was a small frog with two legs in plaster. The car did, however, have a tow bar for attaching trailers at the back. "Right girls, all I need is a bit of twine and I think we can do it."

"We passed an old shack just back there. It's bound to be full of bits and pieces. I'll go and check if you like?" offered Dimity.

"I'll come with you. Lily?"

"Well you won't find anything, so what's the point?"

"Let's go then, Dim. Quick, before the car goes."

They raced to the shack and there, in the corner, was...a pile of twine! Fred grabbed a piece and they hurried back. Carefully he attached one end to the tow bar and the other through a small hole in the bark that had previously been their boat. "Okay, Ladies, take your seats aboard Frédéric's High Speed Skateboard."

"Pas possible! You've got to be joking! It's a death trap; nothing in the whole world would make me go anywhere near it!" scoffed Lily.

"Oh please, Lily," begged Dimity.

"Nothing!"

"Hurry up, there are some people coming and they're heading for the car."

"Nothing!"

"They've turned on the engine."

"Move over you two! Stop being so selfish with space!"

And so the three friends soon found themselves speeding along the road towards Fontainebleau. Cornering proved difficult and at one roundabout, Lily fell against Dimity with such force that Dimity almost fell off the bark. Luckily, Fred grabbed hold of her just in time. He couldn't afford to lose another friend. Kilometre after kilometre flew by and eventually they passed a sign saying 'Fontainebleau 5 km'. "We've got to get off any moment. When I give the word, brace yourselves and hang on tight!" As the car slowed at a bend, Fred unhooked the twine from the tow bar and yelled, "Here we go!" With a series of thuds, the frogs found themselves bumping into the foot of a gnarled, old tree. Not a moment too soon – the car hit an enormous pothole, was launched into the air and then slammed back onto the road with a jolt, sending the small frog from the front bumper flying into the air. Had they been listening, the other frogs would have heard a loud cry from nearby "Not again! Not been my year!" Instead, they blinked and looked around them.

"Hmm, another wood! Whatever next?" Lily asked drily.

"Un instant! Give me a second," answered Fred, "my homing instinct will kick in soon. Then I'll know which way to go and before long you'll be able to meet my mother and everybody." Five minutes later nothing had happened; an hour later and still nothing had happened.

Three hours later Lily piped up crossly. "I thought it was pigeons and not frogs that had a homing instinct. Don't you know anything?"

"Perhaps," Dimity suggested, "we could trek through the woods and hunt for the pond. It should be quite close."

"Don't be so ridiculous. You never have anything worthwhile to say. Personally, I'm fed up with travelling and I certainly don't want to set off in any old direction!"

"Lily, don't be so nasty," Fred was shocked but she just shrugged her shoulders, settled down on some moss and went to sleep. As Dimity watched him faithfully and snuffly snores came from Lily's pretty nose, Fred furrowed his brow and thought. And thought. And thought.

Towards evening, a wind began to build in the treetops and still Lily snored, Dimity watched and Fred thought. An owl hooted in the distance. An idea dawned on Fred. A risk taker's idea. "Venez ici! Hey, Dimity; hey, you too, Snoring Beauty! I've got it – listen to this!" So it was that shortly afterwards, the three of them and the bark were to be found in a leafy glade; the frogs were lying on their backs, the twine more or less securing them to the bark. It was, for all the world, as if they were sunbathing but the sun was low in the sky and had little strength in it. Suddenly, with a triumphant screech, an owl swooped down and picked up the bark and its frogs. Then it flapped its mighty wings and flew silently over the darkening forests, aiming for its favourite feasting tree.

Lily trembled with fear, Dimity waited next to Fred; he was calm. For her, that was enough. As the owl swept through the air, Fred scanned the land beneath, searching for familiar sights. It was a blessing that the owl had been hunting far from its usual haunts for now it had to cover several kilometres with its powerful wings to reach home. Suddenly, Fred spotted the pool in the centre of the wood where his mother Marie had tried to help him conquer his fear of water so long ago.

"Time for us to be off," he cried. With a jerk of his leg, he flicked up the end of the twine, which tied them to the bark so that it whipped into the eyes of the predatory owl. With a squawk of outrage, the bird tried to sweep the twine from out of its eyes. As it did so, its grasp on the bark loosened and slipped. The frogs found themselves falling earthwards but they held on desperately to the bark; then miraculously (as Fred had gambled it would) the bark became a hang-glider.

Yet even as they began to glide through the sky, Lily's tired grip weakened. Before either of her friends could prevent it, she was tumbling towards the ground. Fred reacted in a flash: he tilted the glider downwards and instantly began to pursue the petrified Lily. Fred, Dim and the hang-glider sliced through the air almost out of control. As they came level with Lily, Dimity snatched at her and helped her to secure a firm hold on the hang-glider. "If you ever let me slip again," snapped Lily to Dimity. "You'll be hearing from my lawyers! Fred, mon cher, darling, hold me tightly, I'm so scared."

Using air currents and the strong winds, the frogs regained a little height and then Fred steered them towards the pool. As they drew nearer, so there appeared a beautiful vision – Fred's pond.

Down below in the gloaming a frog, who was enjoying the spectacle of a full moon, saw the hang-glider circle the pond twice before alighting as gently as a feather on the grass beside it. The frog rushed up to it. "Frédéric? Is that really you?"

Chapter 17
The Final Countdown

Fred disentangled himself and the other two from the twine. "Mathieu? Yes, it's me. I'm home." He gave his brother a long hard hug. "This is Dimity and..." Lily pushed her way past the gentle frog. "This is Lily. They've both been brilliant; if it hadn't been for them I wouldn't be here today. Girls, this is one of my brothers, Mathieu."

"Well Mathieu, you can be the first to know; Fred and I are going to be married and Dimity is going to be my maid of honour, aren't you, Dim?" Lily put her arms around Fred and stared dramatically right into his eyes. "My Fred is simply wonderful. And we're desperately in love." Fred blushed deeply while Dimity reeled backwards.

"Well, actually..." Fred stuttered.

"And you Mathieu," interrupted Lily, "can be our Best Man! I hope you're good at making speeches!" With that, she gave her fiancé a kiss and, dragging Dimity behind her, started to move away. "Come on, Dim! Let's take a tour of my future husband's home!"

"Well, congratulations Fred," said Mathieu slapping his brother on the back, "you've got yourself an absolute beauty there, you lucky chap. That other one's a bit plain though! Never mind it's not her you're going be hitched with!"

Fred hesitated for a moment and then gave a huge grin. "Oui mon brave! Yeah, she's stunning isn't she? And she sings and dances too and my word she's athletic. But, Mathieu," a sudden thought seemed to come into Fred's mind, "how's Mum?"

"She's been utterly miserable since you left; she thinks that you're probably dead and she blames herself. She sits around moping all day and nobody can cheer her up. She'll be beside herself with joy to see you. Let's go and find her now."

They walked over to the very edge of the pond where Fred nervously called out: "Mother? Are you there? C'est moi! It's me, Fred; I mean Frédéric." A ripple rapidly came towards the shore and in the middle of it was Marie.

"Here she comes," said Mathieu, "I'll leave you to it."

"Frédéric, I mean Fred! I can't believe it!" Marie gasped as she sprang from the water. "Is that actually you?" She burst into tears.

"Yes, it is. I'm back; I've had some amazing adventures and I've made some great friends but there's no place like home and I'm here to stay. Mum, I'm sorry, I know you were trying to help me. I was such a spoilt frog. And I'm so happy I'm back. I'm still frightened of water, you know? Please don't tell anyone that I'm still not a real frog."

"Oh Frédéric, I wish I hadn't said that! I don't care what makes you scared. I wouldn't mind if you were terrified of butterflies; you're my son and that's all that matters."

Word of Fred's return soon spread amongst the pond-dwellers. The Mathieus organised a splendid party for the next evening to celebrate his homecoming. Frogs from neighbouring ponds were invited and with them came a hobbling creature with three legs encased in plaster. Fred insisted on remaining either in his boat or on a lily pad throughout the evening as Lily splashed around chatting to everybody about their wedding plans. Dimity quietly watched from the shadows of a reed bed.

"Come on Fred," said Isabelle as the moonlight twinkled on the water, "let's go for a swim!"

"I don't think I will if it's alright with you. I'm feeling a little under the weather," responded Fred.

"I don't believe you," Isabelle said scornfully, "I think you're still frightened of water. Once a coward, always a coward!"

"What did you say?" shouted Lily who was just swimming past. "Who's frightened of water?"

"Your precious fiancé, that's who! Scared out of his wits! Who'd want to marry him?"

"Is this true? Have you been deceiving me all this time? I'm humiliated! How could you be so cruel and selfish? And after all I've done for you! How could you lie to me?"

"I never said anything, Lily! I never claimed anything."

"Well, why didn't you tell me? C'est fini! It's over Fred. We're finished. You've let me down," she raged.

"Quite right, Lily," chimed in Isabelle.

"We're sorry about our brother, he's always been different. We don't think he's really a frog at all! Perhaps he's a hedgehog!" laughed Mathieu. "We'll all go for a swim. Fred, why don't you join us in your boat?"

"Thank you, Mathieu, but I'll stay here, I think. I quite like the hedgehog's life!"

"Well, I don't! Where are us real frogs going, boys?" asked Lily. Fred stared at her and shrugged.

Dimity stepped out of the shadows and exploded. "You don't know anything, you lot! Don't you dare talk about Fred like that!" The Mathieus stopped and listened as Dimity described the escape from the tower. Soon Lily edged back towards the group and joined in, re-enacting the dramatic flight from 'The Raw Frog' and then Dimity continued with the tale of the gold medal triumph. More and more frogs gathered to listen and they were all spellbound. On she went to re-create the daring descent into the drains of the stadium; the hunt by the vicious Froghound, Crash; the genius that Fred had shown at the helm of the boat; and finally the scary journey behind the speeding car.

"Donc, so," she finished, "he's not a coward. He's a great frog! He's the truest and best friend I've ever had!" Fred looked at her with a little smile playing on his lips. A tremendous cheer erupted from the audience and then the Mathieus led a chant – FRÉDÉRIC, FRÉDÉRIC, FRÉDÉRIC! Lily sidled up to Fred. "My handsome, talented fiancé; I'm so proud of you! What a terrific pair we're going to make!"

Dimity sadly walked away from the beautiful couple.

"No, Lily! It's not going to happen; you're beautiful but I can't trust you; I never proposed to you in the first place and anyway there's someone else."

"Someone else? Not that little drip Dimity?" Lily was outraged.

"She's not a drip! She's loving, generous and kind and...she makes me happy."

"How ridiculous! Who wants to be happy? I just want to have fun!" Lily snorted. "Oh well, suit yourself! Besides, you're not really my sort; I just felt sorry for you. It's much better that I don't waste myself on you. Good luck with little Miss Boring. See you around!" And off she strutted back to the party. Fred spent all night hunting everywhere for Dimity but, to his despair, he couldn't find her.

The celebrations continued into the early hours with a few foolish frogs becoming just a little drunk on beetle juice. One of them fell off a tree stump. "Bother it! That's the last leg ruined, but crikey what a party!" giggled Jacomo.

The next morning Dimity came back and sat at the edge of the pond, staring pensively at her reflection. She gazed into the distance where she could hear Lily, flirting and singing with the Mathieus. *How could I ever have dreamt that Fred would want to be with me? Who was I kidding? If only I were as pretty and witty and bright as Lily,* she thought sadly, *Perhaps somebody would want to be with me.* She hung her head, tears in her eyes, *Mais non! No, I've made my decision; it's time for me to move on to somewhere else. I'll say goodbye to everyone and be off.* Just at that very moment, an exhausted Fred hopped up. His search was over; he had found her. "Oh thank heavens I've finally found you!" He grinned. "Heh! What's up, Dim?" he asked as he suddenly noticed the expression on her face.

"I'm leaving, Fred. There's nothing here for me."

"What! You can't be serious!" Fred was horrified. "You can't leave me; I need you."

"You don't," she said slowly, "you've got Lily."

"No, I haven't. Didn't you hear what she said last night Dimity? She doesn't want me and to be honest I've never been more relieved in my life."

"But I heard her say that you two would make a beautiful couple!"

"Dimity, immediately after that I told her it wouldn't happen. Anyway, I never asked her to marry me; she invented it all. For a little while, I forgot what she was like but then I remembered; I just didn't know how to tell her. I'm sorry I was so weak. Can you forgive me? You see, it's you Dimity. You're the one that I want and I've known it for ages, but it'll only work," he hesitated, "if you can put up with a coward."

She looked up at him with big eyes. "Of course I forgive you and I've already told you that you're not a coward, Fred."

"But I am, Dimity. You haven't noticed but they were telling the truth: I'm frightened of water. I've always been frightened of water. Imagine that: a frog who's frightened of water. Lily's right. They're all right, I am a coward."

"Fred, I've known for ages. I've seen you near water. And I don't care. Because you're brave in so many other ways and..."

"And?"

"And I love you."

Epilogue

Under the Eiffel Tower in the dank, fetid headquarters of the Bone Suckers, Claude and Clémentine were crouched over a detailed map of Northern France.

"So, that's all the ponds near Vierzon dealt with. Where next?"

"Fontainebleau."